I0093252

The Hinterkaifeck Murders:
Terror in the German Countryside

By

D.A. Chadwick

WordMerchant Publications

Hinterkaifeck: Terror in the German Countryside by D.A. Chadwick © 2023
1st printing 2022 by WordMerchant Publications
2nd printing 2023 by WordMerchant Publications
ISBN 9798987295977
3rd printing WordMerchant Publications
ISBN: 9798987295984

Library of Congress Control Number: 2023922665

Printed in the United States of America

Books by D.A. Chadwick

Deer Creek: The Murders of William
H. Gibson and John S. Frazer The
1st Field Hospital: A Medics
Experiences in the Southwest Pacific God
Barks
Silence is a Lethal Weapon
The Grass Widow: A Civil War Tale The
Singing Nun Story: The Life and Death
of Soeur Sourire
Retribution
Rennes le Chateau: The Road to Sion
The Chimera Project
The Good Nazi
Paper Memories: Distant Voices of the
Third Reich Volumes I and II

Cecilia and Andreas Gruber

Table of Contents

List of Murder Victims

1. Cecilia Gruber (born Sanhüter), widow of Joseph Asam (11/27/1849) born in Gerolsbach). She owned the Hinterkiack farm when she married Andreas Gruber.

2. Andreas Gruber (born 11/09/1858 in Grainstetten). Married Cecilia Asam who owned the Hinterkaifeck farm near Gröbern, Germany.

3. Victoria Gabriel, born Gruber, landlady and widow of Karl Gabriel from Laag, (02/09/1887) living in Hinterkaifeck), and their child

4. Cecilia Gabriel, daughter of Victoria and Karl Gabriel. Born January 9, 1915. Found murdered in the barn. Only child from her marriage to Karl Gabriel (03/04/1914).

5. Joseph Gruber (09/09/1919), illegitimate son, supported by Lorenz Schlittenbauer, neighbor and town spokesman of Gröbern. On 09/30/1919 guardianship was determined at Schroben Court after Schlittenbauer acknowledged paternity.

6. Maria Baumgartner was born on October 1, 1877 as one of six children of married couple Joseph Baumgartner (died 1888) and Maria Baumgartner, born Birner (died 1904), in Kühbach (Swabia) near Gröbern. Three of her five siblings were still alive in 1922. Unmarried Maria Baumgartner lived in her parents'

house in Kühbach until her mother's death. In March 1922 she was placed by an employment agency with Andreas Gruber.

Hinterkaifeck farm April 5, 1922. 1. Residential wing
2. Victoria's room 3. Feeding stalls.

Prologue

March 31, 1922 Near Gröbern, Germany

It was a frigid, snowy day on a farm a few hundred meters from the small village of Gröbern, Germany. Andreas Gruber and his daughter, Victoria, traveled to the town of Schrobenhausen just southwest of their farm for supplies. Their homestead was called, Hinterkaifeck, which simply meant. "behind Kiafeck", a town just south of the farm and forty miles north of Munich.

They each went separate ways with Andreas going to Vogel's hardware store. Though not much of a socializer, Gruber mentioned that he had been hearing strange noises in the attic of his house and one of his cows had been untied and roaming the courtyard. On an earlier trip he also told locals that he was missing his house key. The day before, Gruber had run into his neighbor, Lorenz Schlittenbauer, and told him about footprints coming from the woods that ended at the house. There were no prints leaving the area. He and his daughter also saw a man standing at the edge of the woods near their farm a few days ago just watching them. The thin old man was very nervous, but refused to involve police.

Victoria went to a general store where she too expressed concerns over the odd incidents around the farm. Her father had taken his shotgun up to the attic as they had all heard

9

bumping around up there. He had found no one, but two piles of hay both had dents in them as if someone had been sleeping there. The missing front door key was disturbing to her as well. There was no good explanation for the footprints that vanished at the barn either. Locals also suggested to her that they contact police, but Victoria knew her father would not. The two finished their errands then journeyed by horse drawn wagon back to the farm before bad weather moved in.

A forest known as the Hexenholz (Witches Woods) was fairly large and thick and encircled Gruber property. It was not unusual for people to walk through the woods as a shortcut or take the paths that ran through the forest and around Hinterkaifeck on the way to Gröbern. The farm appeared as if on a triangular shaped island between the dirt roads.

The Hinterkaifeck family spent many hours in the forest cutting wood for the fireplace and ovens. Sometimes, Gruber's wife, Cecilia, remained at home while Andreas, Victoria and her seven-year-old daughter, also named Cecilia (Cilli) trekked to cut firewood. Cecilia would watch Victoria's other child, the toddler Joseph, and baked bread for the trio that would return starving. That afternoon she waited for them to return home from Schrobenhausen anxious about the coming snow.

Andreas and Victoria arrived back at the farm after shopping and performed needed chores beneath a sky filled with heavy clouds. The wind picked up and they hurried to finish before the blizzard began. They were preparing to plant potatoes for a late August harvest.

At around 5:30 pm their new maid, Maria Baumgartner, arrived accompanied by her sister who bid farewell after an hour as she had to cut through the woods to get back to her husband. The sisters had started off from **Kühbach around 3 p.m. that afternoon, which usually was an hour walk, but they got lost. Though Franziska normally looked out for her older** sister because she was mentally slow, she was freezing and waited at the forest edge while Maria went to a remote farm house to ask for directions. A farm hand in the distance released his dog before he realized it was just a woman with a heavy backpack. She asked where Hinterkaifeck was located and the man gave her directions. It was easy as the place was in the middle of a field surrounded by woods. No other houses close by.

The snow was picking up and the temperature was dropping. Maria and Franziska arrived at the farm around 5 p.m. and knocked on the rear door. An older woman answered and beckoned them into the Gruber house. The two travelers warmed up by the fire after Maria hung up her wet jacket near the fireplace. The farmer's wife, Cecilia, was in the kitchen with the two children while their mother and grandfather were still outside in the field. Franziska remained for an hour and left as Victoria Gabriel entered the house. She introduced herself briefly then left for home.

The grandfather, Andreas Gruber, finally came in through the passage from the barn. He was tall, thin and sixty-three years old. The adults sat at the table awaiting dinner while the children went to play near the fireplace. Andreas told her to put her things in the maid's room off the kitchen. Maria did as he told her and placed the rucksack on the windowsill in her new room. The older man motioned for her to sit with him and Victoria while his wife finished cooking a bread soup.

The nearest town was only 500 meters distance yet felt very cut-off to the young maid, probably why it was called, "Eindhof" or isolated. Maria obeyed and sat at the far end of the table. Andreas eyed her in such a way it made her uncomfortable. The young woman briefly wondered about the previous maid who had left abruptly after a few months. The mother of the two children sat to the right of Andreas who

11

headed up the other end of the old wood table. The grandmother, Cecilia, sat next to the toddler, Joseph. The seven-year-old girl, Cilli, sat next to her mother.

The conversation was sparse at first with the two women being very solemn. Victoria, the mother of the two children, had bruises on her face and arms. The Grubers were not used to the new maid and were generally not sociable people, but eventually talked of the weather and some of the past incidents. The day before Andreas had discovered the lock on his engine shed was broken. It was odd, but it did not concern him that much since there was no access to the barn or house from that addition. It still angered him though. His wife, Cecilia seemed very uncomfortable and played with her grandson for distraction.

Cilli had gone to school the day before clearly exhausted and when questioned by the teacher the child explained that her grandfather hit her mother who had then run from the house screaming. Apparently, the adults had engaged in arguments over something that happened and Victoria reached a breaking point. The farmer's wife's thoughts were clearly occupied as she got up to stir the soup.

The old house creaked and groaned with the wind, the snow quickly sticking to the windows. Andreas put another log in the fireplace, which made the flames dance high for a few minutes. The place was dimly lit with oil lamps. It was cold with the windows icing over in spite of being shuttered. The infant, Joseph, was placed in his stroller in his mother's room after becoming sleepy from eating some bread and milk. Little Cilli was allowed to play near the fireplace while they waited for the bread soup to finish cooking.

The house creaked and groaned like an old ship. The attic stairs were between the bedroom of Andreas and Cecilia Gruber and Victoria's room. Their house was L-shaped with

billion or £6.6 billion, roughly equivalent to $442 billion in 2022).

The United States, Britain and France all had certain demands to decrease Germany's military strength and pay retribution for the war damages, especially France, which suffered major destruction to property and lost 1.3 million soldiers or 25% of the 18 to 30 male population.

Adding to the turmoil was the simmering anger of many veterans regarding Germany's surrender when from the troops point of view, they were winning, only to have the Kaiser sell them out. Attitudes against the monarchy were increasingly hostile and the war failed to make desired changes to the government. Many young German soldiers felt betrayed, including Adolf Hitler.

The treaty stripped Germany of 25,000 square miles of territory and 7 million people. It required Germany to give up the gains made via the Treaty of Brest-Litovsk and grant independence to protectorates that had been established. In Western Europe, Germany was required to recognize Belgian sovereignty over Moresnet and cede control of the Eupen-Malmedy area. Within six months of the transfer, Belgium was required to conduct a direct vote on whether the citizens of the region wanted to remain under Belgian sovereignty or return to German control, communicate results to the League of Nations and abide by the League's decision.

In compensation for destruction of French coal mines, Germany was to cede output of the Saar coalmines to France and control of the Saar to the League of Nations for 15 years after which a direct vote would be held to decide sovereignty. The treaty restored the provinces of Alsace-Lorraine to France by rescinding the Treaty of Frankfurt of 1871 regarding this issue. France was able to successfully claim that the provinces of Alsace-Lorraine were indeed part of France and not part of

Germany by disclosing a letter sent from the Prussian King to the Empress Eugénie, in which William I wrote that the territories of Alsace-Lorraine were requested by Germany for the sole purpose of national defense and not to expand the German territory. The sovereignty of Schleswig-Holstein was to be resolved by a direct vote to be held at a future time (Schleswig Plebiscites).

In Central Europe, Germany was to recognize the independence of Czechoslovakia (which had actually been controlled by Austria) and cede portions of Upper Silesia. Germany had to recognize Poland's independence and renounce "all rights and title over the territory". Portions of Upper Silesia were to be ceded to Poland, with the future of the remaining province to be decided by plebiscite (direct vote).

The border would be determined regarding voting and geographical and economic conditions of each locality. The province of Posen (Poznań), which had come under Polish control during the Greater Poland Uprising, was also to be ceded to Poland. Pomerelia (Eastern Pomerania), on historical and ethnic grounds, was transferred to Poland so that the new state could have access to the sea, which is known as the Polish Corridor.

The sovereignty of southern East Prussia was decided via direct vote while the East Prussian Soldau area, which was astride the rail line between Warsaw and Danzig, was transferred to Poland outright without a vote. An area of 20,000 square miles was granted to Poland. Germany was to cede the city of Danzig and its hinterland, including the Vistula River delta on the Baltic Sea, for the League of Nations to establish the Free City of Danzig. Article 119 of the treaty required Germany to renounce sovereignty over former colonies and Article 22 converted the territories into League of Nations mandates under the control of Allied states.

The military mandates were strict, crippling Germany's defenses and deterred further aggressive behavior. Germany was to demobilize the military by March 31, 1920 leaving an army of no more than 100,000 men in a maximum of seven infantry and three cavalry divisions.

The reparations of 132 million gold marks the League of Nations demanded from Germany weakened the economy and contributed to high inflation. The Germans blamed the situation primarily on the Treaty and not prior conditions. With such harsh requirements it was inevitable that there would be another major war. There was no shortage of political upheaval and assassinations in 1922 and Bavaria was a hotbed of terrorist activity. At that time there were many reformation groups with the Deutsche Arbeiterpartei, (DAP), (precursor to the Nazi party), only one of various political movements. Bolshevism and antisemitism were rampant. Someone had to be responsible for the current conditions.

After dissolution of the Wehrmacht (German military) in 1921 these political circles found a new cause in the right-wing extremist scene as they preferred militaristic activities to a legitimate career. This was not a situation unique to Germany or World I. The aftermath of any major war leaves behind soldiers who suddenly have nothing to do or no skills that can be used in civilian life. The times were chaotic and many veterans were still wandering home after being listed as killed or missing in action. There was unemployment with mostly low paying, service-type jobs available.

The police had much to occupy them in March 1922. The more radical political groups kept weapon stashes near Munich and surrounding areas. The Versailles Treaty outlawed civilians from owning weapons, but militant defenders of the fatherland had other ideas. In response, in August 1920 the Reichstag passed a disarmament law requiring the population to report hidden weapons. Maria Sandmayr discovered such a cache at her former employer's residence, Count Fischler von Treuberg at Gut Holzen near Augsburg.

Police files indicate that Sandmayr wanted revenge against her former employer for treating her badly. She might have also hoped there was a reward for turning him in. As a maid she would not have had much of an income. Not knowing how to report the find, Maria tore off the address of the Wallbauer printers on Sendlinger Strasse after reading a poster advising that weapons should be handed in. On September 23 she asked where to report the hidden cache. Instead of being referred to the police, she and a companion were sent to Alfred Zeller, a leader of the local militia. Sandmayr reported to him that there were cannons in the Count's attic and 80 rifles in the cloakroom.

Alfred Zeller then bragged to his colleagues how he had prevented discovery of a weapons cache that a Miss Sandmayr from Odelzhausen sought to report. Another militia officer, Hans Schweighart, learned about the case from Zeller's boasting and after some research located her address. On the evening of October 5, he and two other men drove up to Tengstrasse and asked Sandmayr to get into their car for questioning about the weapons cache of the Nazi party.

On October 6, 1920 two young men came upon a gruesome sight at noon in Forstenrieder Park southwest of Munich. There the slumped over body of a blond young woman was propped against a spruce tree. Her head was tied to the tree with a string. The strangulation marks on her neck indicated the cause of death. A handwritten note made of gray parchment paper hung on the tree above the corpse, praising killing a traitor to the fatherland. The criminal case was the first "fememord" (politically motivated female murder), in the new Free State of Bavaria, and it was also the only known fememord of a woman during the Weimar Republic. The name of the dead woman was Maria Sandmayr.

The murder was still unsolved when Munich detectives had the six murders at Hinterkaifeck fall on their already crowded desks. The police have received much criticism in the years since the murders for their processing of the crime scene and investigation, but the chaotic times come into play as well as transportation and communication issues.

Several local neighbors wandered through the crime scene when the bodies were discovered prior to nearby police departments   arriving,   then   a   judicial   commission   did preliminary inspections before the Munich detectives took over. Things could have been organized better, no question. In hindsight, what occurred seems clear to us, however, on a cold, snowy night when ordered out to the crime scene there was little communication about what had already been done or who had been questioned. There were no two-way radios, few police vehicles, forensics was in its toddler stage and there was no electricity at the farm house. Only later did spotlights, shovels, etc. become part of police standard equipment. Typewriters were state of the art and fingerprinting was not used in all police departments.

Such a multiple murder today would probably have been solved shortly after the crime. DNA alone could have eliminated suspects or sealed the fate of the guilty. But in 1922 German police used what skills and technology they possessed. Even with the present-day media being flooded with true crime shows   and   unthinkable   murders   being   committed,   the Hinterkaifeck story still terrifies people because of the brutality and the fact that is proves you are not safe in the one place people are supposed to feel secure: your home: a still truly scary story for the campfire.

Hinterkaifeck   Chadwick

Hinterkaifeck

20

Chapter Two

Tuesday, April 4, 1922
Hinterkaifeck Farm

On Tuesday morning of April 4, 1922, a 22-year-old mechanic named Albert Hofner was on his way to the small village of Gröbern in Upper Bavaria, Germany with just under 80 residents. He rode a bike through the snow packed roads in response to constant badgering by Andreas Gruber to get to the farm. The Ziegler machine factory, was extremely busy and Albert did not appreciate Gruber complaining to his boss. He did not care for the stingy old fart at all.

Hofner, a stocky dark-haired man, was supposed to repair a stationary engine on the "Hinterkaifeck" farm, which was some 500 meters west of the village. Shortly before 9 a.m., Hofner arrived at the Gruber farm. No one appeared to be at home as the back door was locked and nobody could be seen through the kitchen and barn windows. Hofner waited for an hour then quickly pried open the padlock on the engine shed with a crowbar.

21

The small shed attached to the back of property outside the barn housed the Type H Sendling stationary motor that the mechanic was hired to fix. For the three hours he did repair work, Albert heard nothing more than the dog barking and cows mooing. In order to break the silence and make the time pass, he sang and whistled. When Hofner picked up a nut he had dropped, he had the impression that someone dashed past the engine shed behind him. Hofner emerged from the shed to check, but failed to see anyone. About this time, he realized he would not be getting any lunch or a place by the fire from the Grubers who were not exactly known for their hospitality or generosity. He was not in a good mood.

After repairing the engine, Hofner started it for a short test run at around 2:30 p.m. When even the loud engine noise failed to attract attention from the house, the mechanic closed the engine shed again and walked around the property one last time. The dog was tied up near the front door in the courtyard and barked incessantly. The gate to the engine shed was open. Hofner peered into it a short distance; but did not enter. Since the front door was locked and he could see nobody through the windows to the right or left, Hofner left the farm.

Albert gruffly requested that two young women (Mary and Victoria Schlittenbauer), who worked in the garden of a nearby farm, tell the residents of Hinterkaifeck that the motor had been repaired. He had not been able find the family anywhere. The women, daughters of the local town leader, Lorenz Schlittenbauer, reported what the mechanic told them during a work break.

Lorenz Schlittenbauer then sent his two sons to Hinterkaifeck at around 3:30 p.m. to relay the message. The 16- and 9-year-old boys returned a little later and stated they walked around the courtyard, but did not find anyone.

Schlittenbauer then alerted neighboring farmers, Michael Pöll and Jacob Sigl, and went with them and his two sons to Hinterkaifeck.

Schlittenbauer, Pöll and Sigl entered the barn passage through the unlocked door to the engine shed area and from there gained access to the barn by force. There were corpses lying on top of one another of Andreas Gruber, 67 years old, his wife Cecilia Gruber, 72 years old, their daughter Victoria Gabriel, 35 years old, and 7-year-old Cecilia(Cilli) Gabriel. All victims had severe head injuries; their faces smeared with blood. The gory sight made Pöll and Sigl dash outside for fresh air in the courtyard. Schlittenbauer, who seemed unfettered by the sight and smell entered the living area through the feeding corridor and unlocked the front door from the inside, allowing his neighbors waiting in the courtyard to enter. In the residential wing they discovered the bodies of Maria Baumgartner, a 44-year-old maid, and Joseph Gruber, the two-year-old son of the farm owner, Victoria Gabriel.

The first police officers arrived at the crime scene around 6 p.m. They were accompanied by George Gregers who was mayor of Wangen, a nearby village. He was informed of the crime by one of Lorenz Schlittenbauer's sons. The first investigative authority, a three-person judicial commission from the Schrobenhausen District Court arrived at the property at around 10 p.m.

Prior to arrival of the first police officers, the position of two corpses in the barn had been moved: While the body of Andreas Gruber was pulled down from the pile of corpses and turned on its back, the corpse of Cecilia (Cilli) Gabriel, which had been hidden near the western barn wall, was moved slightly and pulled out of the hay toward the forage cutting machine. The position of the corpses as found by officers of the Munich police in the early morning of April 5, 1922 was not the original location as the afternoon of the previous day, nor did it fit the description from the Judicial Commission from the late evening of April 4, 1922. Local police made an attempt to reconstruct the barn scene with original locations of the bodies.

The "Hinterkaifeck" crime scene was a farm with postal address of field number 564b, Gröbern, house number $27^{1/2}$. Just southwest of the village of Gröbern, the farm was a 4-to-5-minute walk from the village over a slightly sloping dirt road. From Gröbern the road led past the northern side of the property and turned sharply south behind the farm. After approximately 1.2 kilometers the path intersected the local Schrobenhausen-Wangen road. In the western part of Gröbern from Hinterkaifeck the roofs of houses can still be seen sprouting up over a slight hill.

After discovering the crime, Lorenz Schlittenbauer sent his oldest son, Johann, to Mayor George Gregers in Wangen, about 2.1 km away. The mayor notified the police in Hohenwart where the nearest police station was located. On the way to Wangen, Johan Schlittenbauer shouted out to everyone he met that all the residents in Hinterkaifeck had been slain. Numerous people spontaneously rushed to the scene.

It was estimated that Johann Schlittenbauer arrived in Wangen shortly after 5:00 p.m. and informed Mayor Gregers about the ghastly discovery. Around 5:30 p.m., Gregers notified the Hohenwart police either by phone or by messenger from the Brunner Inn in Waidhofen 2.5 km away, where there was a post office with a telephone and telegraph station.

The police in Schrobenhausen were then informed by Hohenwart officials. At around 6:15 p.m., the Munich Police Department and the Public Prosecutor's Office in Neuburg were alerted by telephone and the Munich Police Department was asked to deploy detectives and police dogs immediately.

They had established a evidence dog unit in 1908, now commonly known as K-9 Units.

Mayor Gregers and two police officers, George Goldhofer, Hohenwart Police station commander and Sergeant Major Alois Blank, also headed for Hinterkaifeck. When the men arrived at the crime scene around 6 p.m., there were already dozens of curious onlookers from Gröbern and surrounding areas circling Hinterkaifeck along with Lorenz Schlittenbauer who had discovered the bodies.

At 10:00 p.m. the three-person commission of the Schrobenhausen District Court, consisting of Chief Judge Wiessner, Court Inspector Glaser and Court Assistant Schäfer, arrived at Hinterkaifeck and performed an initial investigation of the crime scene using kerosene lamps. In addition to Mayor George Gregers and the local judicial commission, Schrobenhausen police officers, Johann Anneser and Ernst Grossmann. Sergeant Anneser also conducted a preliminary house search along with their colleague, Grossmann.

The next day the judicial commission returned to Hinterkaifeck, with the second public prosecutor from Neuburg, Theodor Hensold. The Munich police, headed by Chief Inspector George Reingrubers, set off on April 4th, 1922 at 9:30 p.m. with the Munich Identification Service and Criminal Secretary Andreas Biegle. The investigators met Mayor Gregers in Wangen on April 5, 1922 at around 1:30 a.m. because, according to Gregers, a search for evidence at the crime scene was not possible due to the lack of any lighting equipment. The officials waited in the mayor's apartment until dawn then left for Hinterkaifeck at around 5:30 am when Munich detectives began investigating the crime scene.

Throughout the morning, other experts and investigators from the public prosecutor's office in Neuburg arrived. First on the scene was Public Prosecutor Ferdinand Renner, bailiff Heinrich Ney, District Court Coroner Dr. Johann Baptist Aumüller and the owner of the rental car, Schwimmbacherg. Why the police allowed a civilian driver to be involved is not clear. The homicide department at the time did not possess its own vehicle, so perhaps it was policy. The number of police and investigating officers on site can only be estimated due to the conflicting information provided. There were too many.

At least 17 investigators were present on April 5, 1922 creating a preverbal circus. The investigation reports of the Munich police led by Reingrubers and the judicial commission headed by Judge Wiessner laid the ground work for further investigations. There was also a partial record of other incoming reports such as personnel deployed, weather and light conditions, motive for the crime, victims, measurements, photos, sketches, initial conclusions and hypotheses. There was no narration of the changes made at the crime scene after discovery of the bodies.

The first irregularities and screw ups were obvious. Even after the first officials arrived, the crime scene was not secured. In the following years and until the demolition of the farm in February 1923, the crime scene was visited sporadically by investigating officers. During this time, the crime scene was freely accessible, so that in addition to relatives of the victims, numerous crime scene gawkers visited the deserted, haunted farm.

Only five photos of the crime scene were taken, making any accurate reconstruction of the crime scene regarding the body positions impossible. Among other things, the location of Cecilia Gabriel's body cannot be determined based on the photographic material, but can only be guessed at using investigation reports. This is true in most aspects of the case. A clearer picture of the crime is possible only when compiling reports from all police agencies from discovery of the crime until the 1950s.

Footprints at the scene were finally secured by order of the Neuburg public prosecutor, but not until April 8, 1922, four days after the bodies were found. Due to heavy rain and farm field work that had been performed since the bodies were found, the footprints could only be partially preserved. Onlookers visiting the crime scene increased the likelihood that the footprints found were contaminated. According to a forensic investigation of April 8, 1922, footprints from the north-west could not be linked to the crime.

Due to snowfall and rainy weather on April 5, 1922, police dogs could not function as trained. Numerous people entering the crime scene on the day of the incident also decreased any chances of finding evidence using the dogs.

Fingerprint evidence was not saved even though the fingerprint method had been used in the German Reich since 1906. Forensics was still a new technology and not every police department had the equipment or training to gather all evidence. Even typewriters were state of the art in 1922 and not all departments had them or not all officers were trained to use them.

The detectives of the Munich police left the crime scene on April 5, 1922 after ten hours. The property was not systematically examined in the short time available leaving out the attic and barn. Despite the sniffer dogs that were brought along, the murder weapon, a reuthaue (a tool with one side flat and the other like a pick), was hidden in the attic above the residential wing and was not found at that time. At this point, police probably assumed that they had already discovered the weapon in the barn.

According to investigators, the number of victims and other evidence indicated that the crime must have been committed by at least two people. It was theorized that the perpetrators remained in the attic for some time before, during and after the crime. On April 6, 1922, near the eastern entrance gate, the judicial commission discovered a finger-thick rope that reached from the attic to the barn passage floor. The rope was firmly attached to a roof cross beam and used for lifting heavier loads. There were two hand prints on the dusty beam. The rope may have been why Gruber never found anyone in the attic after hearing noises. They had quickly slid down the rope to escape.

In the feeding room, an approximately 1-meter-long pickaxe with brownish-red stains to the eyelet and hoe blade was found, which, according to the investigators' first assumption was blood. This was assumed to be the murder weapon, which made sense as it was close to the bodies.

The attic could be reached from the barn by a wall ladder attached to the west side, which opened over the barn. In the northeastern part of the hay loft above the barn, depressions were discovered in the heaped hay, as if one or more people had been lying there for a long time. There were also stairs from the residential wing up to the attic/hay loft at the opposite end.

Shifted roof tiles were discovered in the southeast corner of the attic above the barn and in the southwest corner of the hay loft. The inner courtyard of the property could be seen through the holes in the attic with views to the south and west where the family could be seen in the fields. The light red color of the roof underneath the shingles indicated that they were only recently moved.

In the smokehouse, which was in the attic above the kitchen near the fireplace, there were nineteen pieces of smoked fish. Half of one piece was cut off. It appeared that someone had been making the attic their living space.

Chapter Three

The Initial Aftermath of the Crimes

Father Michael Haas presided over the funerals on April 8, 1922, which was a rainy, cold and windy Saturday morning. Six black coffins lay near the church wall above the Waidhofen cemetery close to a newly dug mass grave. There were several wreaths of flowers to place on the grave. The coffins were lowered by ropes into the ground by four men as rain drops drummed the wood as if knocking on a door to the afterlife. The dreary, chilly atmosphere was appropriate for the brutalized victims.

The crowd mourned including school teacher, George Sellwanger, who studied the coffin of Cilli Gabriel, who had attended her last day of school. Her short life was over. Her little brother would never even attend school. Hundreds gathered throughout the cemetery despite efforts of police to seal it off.

While the church bells tolled, detectives at the farm worked in the freezing cold to inspect the crime scene and gather evidence. No easy task since numerous people had trampled over the area before police even arrived. Curious citizens still remained watching from a distance while Criminal Commissioner Albert Mayer, an experienced forensic investigator of the Munich Police Department mixed white plaster to pour into two different distinct footprints to make casts. The snow soaked through his pants as he knelt down with George Reingrubers, chief investigator on the case observing. He had ordered Mayer to the scene the night before. Mayer doubted that the shoe prints taken were of the killer as even police had wandered all over the premises, but it was best to be thorough and leave nothing out.

George Reingrubers, had been heading home from his office on Ettstrasse in Munich at 9 p.m. when a uniformed officer on a motorbike flagged him down. He was ordered to return to work and then report to a place called, Hinterkaifeck for a multiple homicide. Reingrubers had a reputation for not giving up on solving cases and was thus a good choice to head up a murder investigation. He was a member of Unit 1 of the Criminal Division, which was responsible for capital crimes in Bavaria. His superiors valued him as diligent and incorruptible, a fit man with a steely expression and a full beard adorning his chin. It would be a long night for him and his men.

At half past nine Reingrubers, George Neuss and Sergeant Hermann Kraus crammed into one vehicle. Two police dog handlers, Sergeant Michael Bohlein and Sergeant Joseph Scheringer and their tracking dogs "Flora" and "Argus" joined them along with Criminal Secretary Andreas Biegleder from the detective division. Biegleder brought unwieldy photo equipment and metal stands for lamps, since he was also responsible for the crime scene photos. It was a long, very uncomfortable ride in blizzard conditions.

It was around 1:30 am when the six Munich officials arrived in Wangen. They were expected by Mayor Gregers who told them he was just back from Hinterkaifeck and with the low light Gregers doubted they would find any evidence. With the snow laden clouds there was no moon or starlight either.

The mayor learned from officials that the judicial commission from Schrobenhausen, which arrived in Hinterkaifeck late in the evening, had already left. Glaser, a court investigator together with assistant Schäfer and court investigator Chief Judge Johann Conrad Wiessner inspected the crime scene. The town representative, Lorenz Schlittenbauer, accompanied them. In the meager light of kerosene lamps and a few stalls with candles, Wiessner, Hans Anneser and Grossmann showed them the individual rooms and the four bodies in the barn. They were especially disturbed by the bloody scene in the baby stroller.

The chief judge instructed the police to keep the lights close by them. Twice he walked the way from the house to the barn and into the barn. Wiessner wondered how the killer managed to lure them there as he saw no bloodstains from the house through to the barn. For a minute he stared at the four dead bodies and decided that they must have been killed right there. "Let's go back the same way that the victims probably came," Wiessner suggested.

The men walked from the kitchen through the hallway and through the feed room to the barn. Wiessner imagined the family moving along the same path. The judge still pondered what could have lured the family into the barn. Were there any calls for help or strange noises? He had two officers go to the barn and scream loudly. In the maid's room and in the combination living and sleeping room of the Grubers, Wiessner strained to hear any calls for help. There was absolutely nothing to hear. The officers tried again, but the walls were too

32

thick and the distance too far. Something else must have occurred that night. The theory was born then that each person was summoned individually by something unknown into the barn and remains a primary theory. It is interesting to note that if screams for help were not heard inside, then how could anyone hear a mooing cow outside in a blizzard, as would later be suggested, luring family members out individually to investigate?

Outside snowflakes drifted steadily downward, not deterring dozens of sightseers who waited outside the farm fence. A mixed group of women prayed the rosary loudly in the glow of flickering candlelight. In a time of no television, few household telephones and radio signals not allowed for Germans due to the Versailles Treaty, such an event would have drawn everyone out in spite of the frigid weather. The ban against radio broadcasts would not be lifted until 1923.

The family dog, Spitz, watched the ordeal with fright and suspicion. With tail tucked between his legs, the yellow dog stayed shyly away from all the men. The chief judge ordered one of the policemen in the house to catch him. The officer had grabbed Spitz when the judge shouted that they needed to leave. Immediately the scared animal snapped at the judge. Wiessner noted that the dog had been wounded on the right eye, which was cloudy and swollen. He later dictated in his report: "Spitz shows great fear, curls up and begins to tremble violently. He cannot be touched."

The commission finally settled in the kitchen. The men were sitting where four days ago the Hinterkaifeckers had been waiting for dinner before being slaughtered. Using the crime scene as a headquarters would never be done today, along with allowing a man who discovered the bodies to wander around with them, regardless of his position as a town leader.

Schlittenbauer should have been treated as a possible suspect, not a tour guide.

Wiessner wondered aloud if it were true that the family was well off. Even before anyone else could answer Lorenz Schlittenbauer stated: "They were comfortable. I reckon that they had around 100,000 marks in cash."

One of the police officers in the house frantically searched for a representative of the Schrobenhausen District Court as there was a man who claimed to have important information. Minutes later the servant, Michael Plöckl, from only two kilometers away in Haidhof, entered the farm house kitchen. It was still being used as an interrogation room. Near Haidhof, Maria Baumgartner had asked for directions and he feared that he had sent her right into the hands of the murderers. Plöckl was asked to describe exactly what he had happened on April 1, 1922.

"Well, at noon on the previous Saturday, which was April 1, I was at Hinterkaifeck. The door to their oven was almost closed all the way. I know that. But when I went back in the evening, it was half-open, just ajar. Also, the fireplace was smoking slightly. It puzzled me, and I turned around, and there was a light at the edge of the forest - it could have been a flashlight." Having said this, he was completely silent for seconds.

"You may have seen the murderers," a police officer stated. "For as you passed by, all six of them had already been dead for hours, and the perpetrators probably still on the farm." Ludwig Meixl from police headquarters at Schrobenhausen lead the witness out. The officials found in a later report that there was no bread left in the whole house. In the smokehouse, twelve pieces of smoked meat hung freshly cut from a half of beef.

It was clear to police that the perpetrators remained in the house for quite some time, and even baked bread, while the corpses were in the bedroom, maid's room and in the barn. "They must have been very sure they would not be discovered," stated Meixl to a colleague. "I'd like to have such nerve. Who knows they still might be around here?"

Chapter Four

Autopsy Results

The district coroner was taking longer than planned as he wanted to dissect only three corpses that first day and the rest the next. Cecilia Gruber had seven mortal blows to her head and her daughter, Victoria Gabriel, had even worse wounds to the same area. Dr. Aumüller counted nine "star-shaped" wounds and on her neck and he found unique strangulation marks. He examined the injuries to her head again and decided that the wounds could have come from the pickaxe, which the Munich detectives took into evidence, but the strange, pencil sized holes in the victims' skull puzzled him. The murder weapon had not been found at this time. Further autopsy of the 35-year-old widow showed that she was not pregnant.

Aumüller had already decapitated the three previously autopsied corpses. The skulls would later vanish after being sent to the Neuburg an der Donau District Court for evidence for future prosecution. From Neuburg they were probably sent to the Augsburg District Court and destroyed there in a night bombing raid by the Allies in 1944 along with many other court records.

The six corpses were autopsied on April 6th and 7th, 1922 at the crime scene on a makeshift table. On the morning of April 6, the bodies of Cecilia Gruber, Victoria Gabriel and Cecilia Gabriel were dissected. The autopsy report of their examinations as well as the autopsies of Andreas Gruber, Maria Baumgartner and Joseph Gruber on the following day are missing in surviving records.

Even if the documents and severed skulls of the murder victims were destroyed by bombs in the war, the fact that no reference is made to an official autopsy report at any point in the further police investigations indicates that outside of notes by the public prosecutor, no comprehensive autopsy report was made at the time. Reports of the public prosecutor's office that have been preserved in the Augsburg State Archives, describe details on the autopsies of the three females, Cecilia Gruber, Victoria Gabriel and Cecilia Gabriel. They are filed with conclusions that detectives reached.

There were seven circular impact marks on the top of Cecilia Gruber's skull along with a three-tang-shaped injury perforating the cranium. The top of the skull was cracked. The Cecilia's face showed severe injuries around her right eye. There are strangle marks on her neck.

The right half of Andreas Gruber's face was damaged with the right cheekbone exposed.

Victoria Gabriel's cranium was shattered and had nine, roughly pencil-thick, star-shaped perforations. The right half of her face had been smashed with a blunt object. She also had strangulation marks on her neck. Victoria Gabriel was not pregnant at the time of death.

The top of little Cecilia Gabriel's skull was smashed and she bore a transverse, gaping wound on her neck, directly below the lower jaw. The neck injury was the cause of the girl's death. Cecilia Gabriel lived an estimated 2 to 3 hours after the crime. She was found clenching her own hair in her closed fist, which was assumed the girl tore out in agony.

There were injuries on Maria Baumgartner's skull that suggested a sequence of cross-strokes from the front, left to right, with a blunt tool. The back of her head had a blood-filled hole some 4 cm deep.

On Joseph Gruber's head there were blow injuries that cracked the skull. Judging by the injury, the blow was made in the middle of the child's face with a striking tool. No defensive wounds were found on any of the six victims.

The six headless bodies were buried on Saturday, April 8th, 1922 in the cemetery in Waidhofen. The heads were prepared and later the craniums brought to two clairvoyants in Nuremberg for their interpretations of events.

The assumed murder weapon, the pickaxe supposedly owned by Schlittenbauer, was initially found when the property was searched. Only when the farm was demolished in February 1923 by the new owner, Joseph Gabriel, was a mattock (Reuthaue) discovered in the false floor above the kitchen near the fireplace. After results of the criminal investigation, human blood and hair remains were on the tool. The mattock can be connected to the crime with near certainty. According to autopsy results, the weapon was a special tool and was designed and made by Andreas Gruber himself with a protruding screw and a nut on an iron plate attached to the blade.

The distinctive screw connection on the blunt side of the blade was the cause of the round, star-shaped head injuries identified during the autopsies of Cecilia Gruber and Victoria Gabriel, as well as the three-tang injury.

Chapter Five

Observations of the Crime Scene Photos and Detective
Reports

The observations below were taken from the crime scene
photos of the detective division of the Munich criminal police
and police reports. The official sources are listed in the
Appendix.

The bodies of Andreas Gruber, Cecilia Gruber, Victoria
Gabriel and Cecilia Gabriel were found on the threshing floor
in the barn. Several of the deceased were piled on top of each
other in the north-western corner of the barn directly in front of
the door to the feeding passage.

Andreas Gruber was lying on his back with his head
directly against the western wall of the barn. The dead man's
skull shows severe injuries. The face was covered with blood
and described as "shredded". Gruber's legs were stretched out.
The arms were slightly angled. The right hand was closed with

the index finger slightly spread and the left hand open. Both hands were on his stomach
   On the little finger, on the back of the right hand and on both feet, dark colorations indicate (lividity) and the feet of the dead appear swollen.

The bodies of Andreas and Cecilia Gruber.

   The dead man wore long, light-colored underpants (thermal underwear?) and a light-colored, long-sleeved shirt extending to his thighs. The right shirt sleeve was buttoned. In the right knee area, the underwear we heavily soiled or darkly discolored.
   Immediately next to the corpse of Andreas Gruber, between the body and western wall of the barn, textiles or fabric remnants were found. There was also a printed cardboard box or a newspaper page.

Body of Victoria Gabriel

A wooden handle protruded from the left towards the center of the picture in both crime scene photos. Below the handle, level with Andreas Gruber's knee, the curved handle of a metal harvest basket or potato basket is visible, and below it the metal basket itself. The second basket handle is right next to the dead man's right knee.

The body of Cecilia Gruber was found lying on her back just right of Andreas Gruber prior the crime scene reconstruction. The body was stretched out and pointed toward the north barn wall. Her head lay directly on the staircase leading to the barn door.

Severe injuries were clear on Cecilia Gruber's skull. The face was covered in blood. The dead woman's right arm was bent, her forearm on her chest. The right hand was half open. The left arm stretched away from the body at a 30° angle. The left leg crossed over the right leg.

The corpse was dressed in a half-sleeved, oblong striped smock apron. The skirt was slipped up so that both knees are exposed. Dark long knee socks can be seen, which are held below the knees by garters. The dead woman is wearing a wooden slipper on her right foot. The skirt part was stained dark over a large area on the left front; A dark color (blood?) can also be seen on the hem of the skirt.

The body of Victoria Gabriel lay on its back, butting against the body of Cecilia Gruber at a 90° angle with Victoria Gabriel's head hidden under the hem of Cecilia Gruber's skirt. The cranium had severe injuries with the face smeared with blood. The right half of the face was also smashed in. The dead woman wore a half-sleeved, striped smock apron and stockings. Shoes were not found. The apron was stained on the right elbow. There were dark spots on the back of the right hand. About 50 cm southeast of Victoria Gabriel's corpse you can see a larger puddle of dried blood on the barn floor.

When discovered the body of Cecilia (Cilli) Gabriel lay parallel to the western barn wall near the barn door in about knee-deep heaped hay. The corpse was also found with hay over it. Severe injuries are visible on her skull and the face covered with blood.

On the girl's neck just below her chin there is a transverse, gaping wound. A circular injury was visible on the right side of the face next to her nose. Cecilia Gabriel was only dressed in a nightgown.

In the reconstructed location of the body, it is obvious judging by the underwear and physiognomy, a male corpse was lying prone with its head towards the northwest barn door. The male body was covered with a light-colored door and a loose layer of hay 30-40 cm deep, so that the upper part of the torso and the head cannot be seen. From the lower back down, the right forearm and both legs protrude from under the door. The right arm lay against the body with the legs straight and parallel to each other. Dark discoloration can be seen on the heel of the left foot and on the outer instep of the right foot. A single wooden slipper lay in the hay about 30-35 cm from the dead man's left calf.

Between the right hand and torso of Andreas Gruber you can see part of a forearm half covered with fabric. About 30-40 cm from the dead man's right wrist, further textile material can be seen through the layer of hay. On the barn side of the wooden door to the feeding passage there was significant blood splatter.

One of the three witnesses who discovered the bodies, Lorenz Schlittenbauer, entered from the barn through the barn into the living area of the property. In the maid's room he found the corpse of Maria Baumgartner lying on the floor in front of her bed. In Victoria Gabriel's bedroom Joseph Gruber was found dead in his stroller.

The following observations were made regarding the crime scene photos following the route investigators took through the scene beginning in the barn, then through the kitchen, maid's room Victoria Gabriel's room and finally the bedroom of the Gruber couple: From the book by Dr. Guido Golla, "Autopsie eines Sechsfachmordes".

1. The farm dog (Spitz) is tied up in the barn. An injury can be seen on the dog's head (swelling and clouding of the right eye).
2. The animal appears frightened.
3. The feeding alley in the barn looks swept up.
4. Individual blood stains are visible on the stone pavement in the kitchen.
5. In the first exit, near the kitchen door, there is another blood stain on the floor.
6. Leftovers and Cecilia Gabriel's school blackboard lie on the kitchen table. There is an enamel bowl filled with bread soup on the stove.
7. Maria Baumgartner's body is found in the northwestern part of the residential area, in the maid's room. The room is approx. 8-9 square meters and can only be entered through the kitchen.
8. The door to the maid's room is open.
9. The maid's corpse lies in the middle of the room on the wooden floor. When found, the dead woman is covered with a plaid bedspread of the single bed in the room. Only the feet,

clad in lace-up boots, protrude from under the covers.

10. As can be seen after pulling down the bedspread, Maria Baumgardner is lying on her side with her face to the door on the floor (although the dead woman's face cannot be seen in the crime scene photo). The dead woman is fully clothed. She wears a patterned skirt and jacket.

11. The legs of the dead are drawn up slightly. The right arm sticks out from the quilt and is angled towards the ground; the right hand is turned inwards with the back of the hand resting on the floor. The left forearm rests on the floor below the chest. The back of the hand points downwards and is slightly raised; the fingers of the left hand are curved inward.

12. The head of the corpse is at the head of the bed. Impact injuries can be seen on the skull; As a result of the injuries, the blows were hit crosswise, i.e., with an alternating direction of impact (left / right). The dead face is smeared with blood.

13. The upper body of the corpse lies in a coagulated pool of blood.

14. A cloth or scarf lies on the floor in front of the corpse. A slipper can be seen to the right under the bed. A woolen blanket hangs on the foot of the bed. The pillow is in the middle of the bed.

15. There are pieces of clothing on the windowsill across from the entrance door. Other items of clothing as well as the travel bag/ rucksack of the dead lie on a wooden bench

below the window. An umbrella is leaning against the wall to the left of the wooden bench.

17. On a shelf on the south wall of the room are saucepans, tin dishes and a labeled paper bag containing 250 g of lead shot. Behind the shelf, in the south-western corner of the room, is a wooden barrel; In front of the shelf, to the left of the door to the kitchen, you can see a cupboard.

18. The house corridor leads through the kitchen to the bedrooms of the Gruber couple as well as Victoria Gabriel and the children. The Gruber couple's bed is unused.

19. Joseph Gruber's body is found in Victoria Gabriel's bedroom. The door to the room is closed, but not locked when it is found. The key is in the outside (doorway side)

20. The two shutters are closed.

21. A few steps behind the door of the approx. 20 to 25 square meter room, a stroller is parked in front of a double bed. The damaged folding roof of the stroller points towards the window side (south). On the folding roof of the stroller lies a dark red dress that reaches down to the wheels.

22. Joseph Gruber's body lies on its back in the stroller. The child's right temple is smashed in. As a result of the force of the blow, blood and pieces of tissue go beyond the inside of the stroller to the foot section of the double bed and are stuck there.

23. There are more blood stains on the floor near the door.

24. The head of the double bed is on the east wall of the room. To the left of the double bed is a

sideboard / writing desk. The shelves in the upper part of the chest of drawers are filled with numerous containers and utensils that have not been recorded in detail. The drawers under the shelves are closed. The two doors of the lower part of the cabinet are slightly open.

25. On the north side of the room there are 3 wardrobes, which appear to be partially open. Blood splatter are not recognizable on the wardrobes. To the left of the front door, with the narrow side on the western wall of the room, is the metal lattice bed of Cecilia Gabriel.

26. Victoria Gabriel's double bed is unused. The duvet is pressed in on the side facing the commode. On this half of the bed, covered by the quilt, lie an empty wallet, a ladies' wristwatch, a notebook, several final notes and written pages of paper.

The maid's room showing her body under the blanket in the center of the picture. Her left hand is visible. Initially, some believed that Maria Baumgartner was the prime motive behind the murders, but this is not likely.

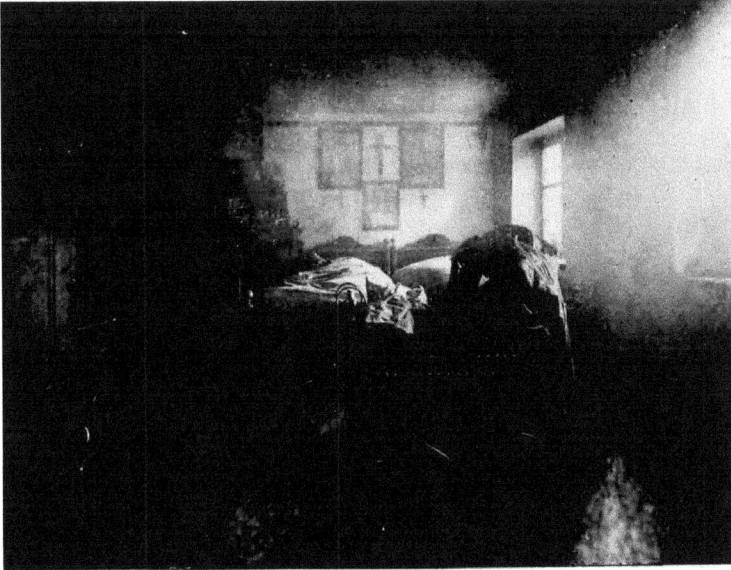

Victoria Gabriel's room showing the stroller in the foreground bearing the dead body of the toddler, Joseph Gruber. Note the bed is still made.

View of Hinterkaifeck from the south showing the residential, feeding stalls and barn sections of the building. The tool/wood shed is on the left.

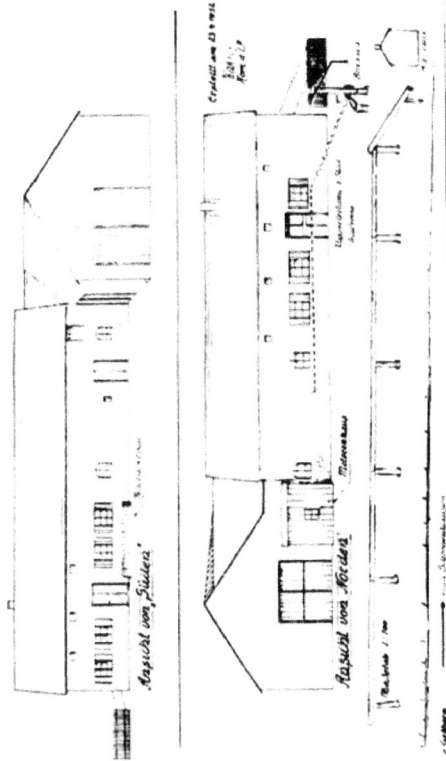

Sketch of Hinterkaifeck by Andreas Schwaiger showing the south (left) and north (right) sides of the building. The engine shed is right of the barn doors.

Karl Gabriel, Victoria Gruber's husband listed as killed in action in 1914. Some believe he was in Gröbern in 1918 and later joined the Russian army after murdering the six people.

Lorenz Schlittenbauer, the closest neighbor to the Hinterkaifeck farm. He was dismissed as the killer by police primarily due to his asthma, which could have been severe and may have been caused by exposure to mustard gas.

Possible photo of Cecilia (Cilli) Gabriel from a class photo. She was seven years old when murdered.

Class photograph circa 1921. Cazillia Gabriel is reported to be the girl center in sailor suit. The class photo with Cecilia Gabriel is said to have appeared in 2008. Georg Sellwanger is the teacher.

A sketch of the farm building showing the individual sections and location of the corpses.

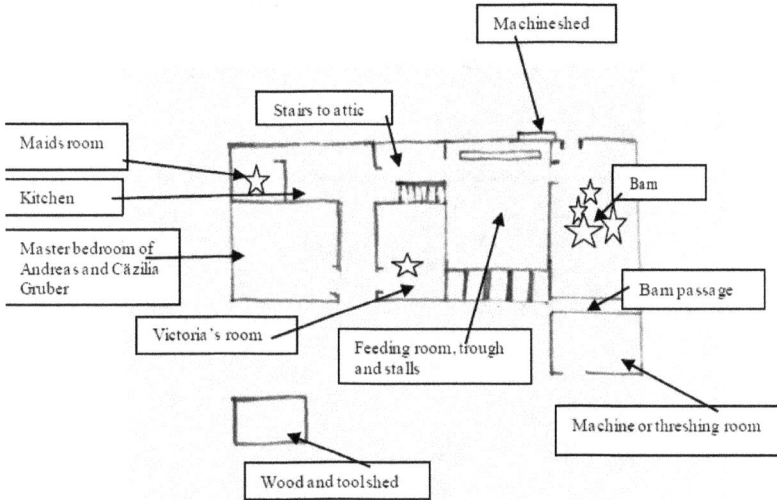

Machine shed

Stairs to attic

Maids room

Kitchen

Master bedroom of Andreas and Cäzilia Gruber

Victoria's room

Feeding room, trough and stalls

Barn

Barn passage

Machine or threshing room

Wood and tool shed

☆   = Location of bodies

Hinterkaifeck   Chadwick

Coffins of the six murder victims April 8,1922

Lorenz Schlittenbauer (far right) was suspected throughout his life of having murdered the Gruber family on the Hinterkaifeck farm. Photo circa 1921.

Troops in France with Raiding or Trench clubs embedded with hob nails. Both German and French troops used them. Some believe Karl Gabriel could have returned from the war and killed the family with such a weapon.
https://www.wearethemighty.com/popular/6-things-about-trench-clubs/

Chief Inspector Georg Reingrubers 1920. The murders
of Hinterkaifeck haunted him long after retirement, yet
he did not mention the case in his memoirs.

Father Michael Haas performed the funerals on April 8, 1922. He also found the 700 gold marks in the confessional at Waidhofen left there by Victoria Gabriel.

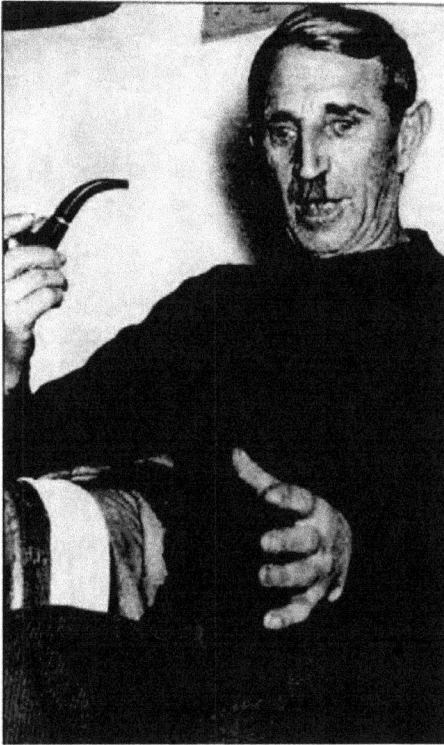

Jacob Sigl discovered the bodies in the barn with two
other neighboring farmers on April 4, 1922.

Mailman Josef Mayer who handed Andreas Gruber the newspaper on Friday, March 31, 1922. This would become an issue as the paper was found stuck in the window sill on discovery of the bodies, April 4, 1922.

Private Karl Gabriel in 1914 in the 6th Bavarian Infantry Regiment. He was listed as killed in action in France.

Chapter Six

The Investigation Advances

The Munich police and judicial commission began interrogating witnesses on the morning of April 5, 1922. After Mayor George Gregers had been questioned by the Munich police on the night of April 4th to 5th, 1922, the three witnesses Schlittenbauer, Sigl and Pöll and the coffee dealers, Hans and Eduard Schirovsky followed.

On Saturday, April 1st, 1922, Franziska Schäfer, sister of the murdered maid, Maria Baumgartner, who accompanied her sister to the property on March 31st, 1922 was questioned along with Bernhard Gruber, brother of the slain Andreas who had tried to place an order for coffee at Hinterkaifeck for Gruber.

The last witness to be questioned that day was

Joseph Schratzebarner from Gröbern, a former servant at Hinterkaifeck. The witness statement was typed on the portable typewriter in the farm house kitchen. All the while the crime scene was visited and surrounded by gawkers until late afternoon. The first rumors began to circulate that the perpetrator (s) were local and they must have been familiar with agriculture because the cattle were fed even after the murders.

Many persons who should have been questioned were not until much later or not at all. The mechanic, Albert Hofner was interviewed two years later and many others not until 1943 or later. Some contradictions in statements could have been noted and acted on earlier. Hofner stated that he had to break the latch on the engine shed to get in and Schlittenbauer said the lock was intact when he found it. Hofner also stated the dog was tied to the front door and Schlittenbauer said the dog was locked in the barn. Either one or the other was lying or the killer could have changed the crime scene before police involvement.

The classmates of seven-year-old Cilli should have been interviewed as well. The child may well have told classmates about her home life. How often did the child miss school? How often was Cilli sleepy at school? Did she tell other students about domestic violence at home and between whom? Did she ever talk about people being in the cellar? Did authorities ever question the school administration regarding Victoria's siblings, did they ever attend school? Do they have any records of such children at all?

The postman, Mayer, stated that he had personally handed the newspaper to Andreas Gruber, but Schlittenbauer's sons found the paper in the window where it was usually placed when they were not home or in the fields. This was an important clue indicating that whoever staged the crime scene was familiar with the victims' habits.

It would have been useful to question the family of Karl Gabriel for further background on the dynamics of the Gruber household as well. He clearly was aware of the father/daughter incest and had disturbing information on the other children kept in the cellar. Children who did not survive and Karl stated that he too was poorly fed by the Grubers. The situation was bad enough that the married man went home to his parents. Today police and social services would investigate the fate of the other children. How many were there that did not survive? Why were they kept in the cellar and for how long?

Though the farm owned by Victoria Gabriel was consistently referred to as "Einodhof" or isolated, it really was not as Gröbern is within a short walking distance and situated between two dirt roads that go around it. Travelers frequently passed the property when the Grubers lived there. The farm was surrounded by a forest called the "witch's wood", where people often short cut through the property. The distance to the forest edge was about 180 meters east from the Hinterkaifeck wood and tool shed to the south some 50 to 60 meters.

The villagers and locals in the Gröbern area probably knew much more than they told investigators about the Grubers and other neighbors. They were particularly cautious about criticizing Schlittenbauer who as a person in power could cause them problems with other residents. He was not challenged concerning the fact that he opened the door inside Hinterkaifeck with a key Andreas Gruber stated was missing. Even Schlittenbauer admitted there was only one. So how and where did he get it? His neighbors would later state that he had many skills and was capable of making one.

****

The Days Before the Murders

In the last week of March 1922, Andreas Gruber reported to neighbors, and people at the Vogel hardware store in Schrobenhausen, that he had discovered footprints in the snow that led to the barn, but no prints leaving there. At the gate or on the outer barn door there were also some signs of burglary, as recorded by the Neuburg Public Prosecutor's office. Gruber also mentioned hearing footsteps in the attic. He had checked out the suspicious noises, but could not find anything unusual in the attic. He and Victoria also saw a man at the edge of the woods watching them working in the field.

Though neighbors suggested notifying the police, Gruber allegedly refused to involve them pointing out that he was able to deal with the problem on his own. His aversion to the police was probably related to the recent arrest for incest. Gruber asked the postman whether someone in the area had subscribed to the newspaper, "Münchner" Zeitung, because he had found a copy in the nearby forest. Since the residents of Hinterkaifeck were considered withdrawn and loners, none of the residents thought to follow up on what happened to them when they had not been seen for several days and even after hearing about the odd occurrences.

The Gabriel/Gruber family were considered wealthy and thrifty with some calling them stingy. So it is curious that Victoria Gabriel borrowed some 5,000 marks from her half-sister, Cecilia Starringer, in October 1921 and 3,000 marks in February 1922. Apparently, the money was needed for pending renovation work on the farm for construction of a new barn and purchasing a threshing machine. In police photos the iron pillars Andreas bought at the hardware store are visible, so those plans seemed to be true. Victoria also closed her savings account, which contained around 1,800 marks, and sold a bank bond worth 3,800 marks. Victoria Gabriel cashed in over 13,000 marks in the last 6 months before her death. She would have owned around 400 to 500 gold marks and 12,500 paper marks at that time, which has a current exchange equivalent to a total of around 8,500 to 9,000 EUR.

The purpose for needing cash could not be determined during the police investigation. It was certain that Victoria Gabriel anonymously placed 700 gold marks in the confessional of the Waidhofen parish church some fourteen days before the murders. Father Haas was familiar with the financial situations of his parishioners and guessed that only the Gabriel/ Gruber family could be considered the donor. He sent a message through little Cilli Gabriel that Victoria should pay him a visit. In an interview with Father Haas, Victoria was said to have admitted after some hesitation that she had put the gold money for the parish mission in the confessional. The reasons for the gift and account closing raised much speculation by police and civilians.

Police used the following information to determine the date of the crimes.

In the early evening of March 31, 1922, the new maid, Maria Baumgartner, arrived at Hinterkaifeck, accompanied by her sister. The sister bid goodbye around 6:00 p.m. On Saturday, April 1st, 1922, Cecilia Gabriel was absent from school in Waidhofen unexcused. She had attended classes on Friday, March 31st, 1922.

The coffee dealers Eduard and Hans Schirovsky visited the property on Saturday, April 1st, 1922. They knocked on the window and peered into the living room, but did not see anybody.

On Sunday, April 2nd, 1922, the Gabriel/ Gruber family did not show up for mass in Waidhofen. Monday, April 3rd, 1922, Cecilia Gabriel again had an unexcused absence from school.

When the bodies were found there was a note on the tear-off calendar in the kitchen for April 1, 1922.

Police fixed the time window for the murders on the evening of March 31, 1922 between 8:00 p.m. and 11:00 p.m. Considering the victims' bed clothes and other observations indicating a time period after dinner or shortly before going to bed. This was assuming a regular day's routine on the farm.

Chapter Seven

Witnesses and Suspects Interviewed

The following statements were taken from the Munich police interrogations from 1922 to 1953.

Lorenz Schlittenbauer
Interviewed April 5, 1922

Farmer and town representative in Gröbern, Lorenz Schlittenbauer (Born 16/08/1874 in Gröbern, died 22/05/1941) was interviewed by police detectives one day after the bodies were discovered on April 4, 1922. Victoria Gabriel had given birth to an illegitimate child, Joseph Gabriel, whom he admitted he was the father. The issue of the child being illegitimate was considered a motive due to jealousy and also inheritance matters, so the topic reoccurred often.

On Saturday, April 1, 1922, around lunchtime, a coffee merchant, from whom the witness's wife regularly ordered coffee, came to Schlittenbauer's property. The dealer told family members that nobody was around at Hinterkaifeck. On Tuesday, April 4th, 1922, a mechanic came to Schlittenbauer's farm and asked the witness's daughter, Victoria Schlittenbauer, to tell old Gruber that the engine had been repaired. The mechanic had seen no one at Hinterkaifeck and everything was locked up. Schlittenbauer heard the stories at Vesper time around 3:00 to 4:00 p.m.

According to Schlittenbauer's stepson, Joseph Dick, Cecilia Gabriel had been absent from school on Saturday, April 1, 1922. The witness sent his sons, Johann Schlittenbauer (16 years old) and Joseph Dick (9 years old), to Hinterkaifeck to knock on the windows and look into the rooms to see if anybody was in the house. The two boys had been instructed to tell the residents that the engine had been repaired.

A short time later his sons returned stating that they had not found anyone at Hinterkaifeck and that the cattle in the barn "bellowed". Then, according to Schlittenbauer, he had his neighbors, Michael Pöll and Jakob Sigl go with him to Hinterkaifeck. This was around 5 p.m. All entrances to the property were found locked, with the exception of the door leading to the engine shed. According to Schlittenbauer, the gate from the engine shed to the threshing floor was locked in such a way that a rod from the gate to the post was firmly attached to the inside of the gate.

He had ordered the gate to be opened to the outside. The three of then entered the threshing floor where a manual chopper stood in the middle. The door to the barns was open and a cow peeked from the barn through the door. Schlittenbauer claimed to have gone ahead to the barn door where there was hay stored in front of the door. He stepped on the hay and stumbled slightly, which he ignored. Pöll who followed him shouted, "There's a foot!", prompting Schlittenbauer to turn around. He grabbed the foot and pulled it to the corner. He recognized Andreas Gruber's foot. The witness then looked more closely around the barn and noticed that other people were lying on the floor. He then pulled Andreas Gruber and Cecilia Gabriel out of the hay. He had laid Cecilia Gabriel about 1.5 meters toward the chopping machine, which was used to cut forage.

Schlittenbauer believed that his son, the 2 1/2-year-old Joseph, might still be alive in the house. He then hurried through the feeding corridor to the residential wing to look for the boy. In the barn Schlittenbauer had to avoid the untied cow and climbed into the feeding trough. A pickaxe leaned against the wall in the feeding room. The witness then went to the kitchen and from there to Victoria Gabriel's bedroom. There he found his son Joseph with a shattered skull in the stroller. He then opened the front door for his two companions, who were waiting in the courtyard. Schlittenbauer then went to the maid's room. There was a blanket on the floor. He lifted the blanket and discovered a female corpse underneath. The person was unknown to him. All three witnesses left the house shortly afterwards.

While Pöll and Sigl went back to Gröbern, Schlittenbauer stayed near the property. He had given his son, Johann, instructions to ride his bike to Mayor Gregers in Wangen and to report the murders at Hinterkaifeck. In the meantime, several farmers from Gröbern arrived at the Hinterkaifeck farm. Around

6:00 p.m., Schlittenbauer ordered the farmer's son, Alois Schwaiger, who was related to the witness, Andreas Schwaiger from Gröbern, to go to Waidhofen and arrange for relatives of the victims to be notified by telephone. In the meantime, several people from the area had come to Hinterkaifeck, but Schlittenbauer did not allow anyone to enter the living rooms or the house. He then fed the cattle. After the police and mayor arrived, Schlittenbauer backed off and let police take over.

 Schlittenbauer added that Andreas Gruber had shouted out to him from the field that on Thursday, March 30, 1922, around 11:00 a.m. he had been stalked by burglars. Gruber had followed tracks in the new snow that led to the property, but could not find any tracks that led away. Gruber noticed that the lock on the door of the engine shed had been pried open. The burglars were in the engine shed, but did not steal anything. There were also indentions made by prying tools on the feed room gate.

 According to Schlittenbauer, the Gabriel/Gruber family was well off. He estimated that there were around 1,00,000 marks in cash in the house and that coins were also in the family's possession. The Hinterkaifeckers, also owned Pfandbriefe (bonds) from various banks. r, the Gabriel/Gruber family lived in seclusion and kept everything locked up. In his second questioning in March 1931 at the police headquarters in Munich, Schlittenbauer stated that he had known the Gruber family since he was born.

 The witness stated that the Gruber couple had several children, but only one daughter, Victoria, survived. The children probably all died because they had no care and were not adequately fed. Schlittenbauer himself and his father had often seen that the children were locked in the cellar for days, and when one walked past the property children could be heard crying in the cellar. "To be quite frank, those people weren't good", Schlittenbauer remarked to police also stating that God had a hand in rectifying it.

Karl Gabriel once complained to Schlittenbauer that he was being treated badly at Hinterkaifeck. The Gruber couple were so stingy that there was nothing to eat at lunchtime. It was also said that the marriage between Karl and Victoria Gabriel would end in divorce. It was common knowledge that Andreas Gruber had sexual intercourse with his daughter Victoria. At the age of sixteen Victoria Gruber became her father's sexual partner. She had told Schlittenbauer that she could no longer hold out against her father because he always wanted to have sexual intercourse.

Schlittenbauer recalled that after the death of Karl Gabriel, criminal proceedings against Andreas Gruber and Victoria Gabriel were initiated and both were convicted of incest. Schlittenbauer stated that Victoria Gabriel was "easy". Shortly after the death of Karl Gabriel, she offered herself to him when they transported a cupboard together on a wagon. The witness did not respond at the time because he was married. After the death of his first wife, Victoria (born 10/15/1869, died 07/14/1918) Victoria Gabriel met him in his hay barn and suggested that he marry her. His wife had only died 14 days earlier. At that time, he did not deny her because he needed a woman around on his farm. Victoria Gabriel also offered sexual intercourse without Schlittenbauer having expressed any interest.

She grabbed him and threw them both on the hay, and that was how Schlittenbauer had sex with her for the first time. In the period that followed, this happened a few more times. One time while she passing it out, Victoria Gabriel repeated the desire to marry him and took him to the barn where she asked him for sex. He added to the record in 1931, "Up until then it had never happened to me that a woman offered herself like this". Schlittenbauer claimed to have had no more than five conversations with Victoria Gabriel.

Victoria Gabriel once suggested to Schlittenbauer that he should speak to Andreas Gruber about getting married. Afterwards it turned out that Victoria Gabriel was already pregnant at the time, but hadn't told Schlittenbauer about it. However, the witness assumed that he could marry Victoria Gabriel, which was why he made a corresponding proposal to Andreas Gruber. Gruber had agreed. Schlittenbauer made it a condition that the sexual intercourse between father and daughter must cease. Gruber was supposed to be saved from his sins, and Schlittenbauer wanted to "lead Victoria on the right path".

Schlittenbauer told Gruber that he was a good Christian and couldn't stand such things, to which Gruber replied: "We'll see then." A short time later, Victoria Gabriel confessed to him that she was pregnant. She claimed that Schlittenbauer was the father, he then replied that her father could well be too. Victoria replied that marriage was the best solution. She could tell Andreas that the child could be his, but he would kill her. She also said that Andreas Gruber was no longer happy with the marriage idea, but that Schlittenbauer still had to be the child's father.

Schlittenbauer confronted Andreas Gruber, but Gruber insisted that Schlittenbauer must recognize paternity. The witness then turned to Cecilia Gruber and Victoria Gabriel again, and they also insisted that Schlittenbauer had to be the father. The two women had also told him that he had to pay child support. Originally, Victoria Gabriel told Schlittenbauer that he did not have to pay anything, but only had to acknowledge his paternity.

After rough treatment by Andreas Gruber and demand for palimony payments, Schlittenbauer filed a complaint on September 10, 1919 for incest, and Andreas Gruber was taken into custody on September 13, 1919 due to repeated offenses.

Schlittenbauer stated that Victoria Gabriel visited him on the third day after the birth (09/10/1919) and offered that she would pay all the money for establishing paternity if Schlittenbauer acknowledged paternity. When asked, the witness stated that he had received 2,000 marks from Victoria Gabriel. After fixing the child support at 1,800 marks, he would have to pay the difference of 200 marks. As Schlittenbauer stated when asked, he had also received three bank notes from Bayerische Hypotheken- und Wechsel-Bank for 3,000 marks in order to be able to pay possible expenses. The witness also voluntarily returned the bank notes after a few months. Since Victoria Gabriel had mentioned that it was still possible to get married, Schlittenbauer agreed.

When Andreas Gruber was imprisoned from September 13, 1919, Victoria Gabriel went to Schlittenbauer and asked him to help her father out again. Since Victoria Gabriel sobbed dramatically, the witness was persuaded and revoked his statements denying paternity. At this point in time, Schlittenbauer was still in possession of the money.

During the judicial interrogation, Lorenz Schlittenbauer stated, when he was to be sworn in, that his revocation was based on false information.

Ultimately, according to Schlittenbauer, he did not have to pay any money out of his own pocket for recognition of paternity, for which Victoria Gabriel even issued him a written confirmation at the time. The witness kept it until the note was destroyed in the fire of the Schlittenbauer family's house in 1926.

Schlittenbauer claimed to have had these discussions with Victoria Gabriel at his residence. The first time was at night so, that no one could see them. The other meetings were during the day. The witness stated that he had no recollection of having asked immediately after the murder whether he would get the severance payment back. Schlittenbauer claimed to have been annoyed about the "murky" paternity issue. His eldest son in particular reproached him.

The descriptions by Schlittenbauer regarding discovery of the corpses on April 4th, 1922 coincided with statements of April 5th, 1922. Schlittenbauer added that he had entered the inside of the house from the barn because he had thought that Joseph Gruber "must be starving". He opened the front door from the inside with the house key in the lock. Schlittenbauer could not explain why the key was in the lock, although Andreas Gruber had reported to the witness before the murder that he had lost the key and that he could only lock the front door with the bolt. Schlittenbauer swore that there was only one house key for Hinterkaifeck. In his opinion, since the door was locked from the inside, the perpetrators left the house with a rope that hung from above in the engine shed. You could go through the attic to the engine shed area and from there let yourself down on the rope.

Schlittenbauer was unable to provide any information about the presence of choke marks on the neck of Cecilia Gruber or Victoria Gabriel, since, as he said, he did not look at the corpses closely.

After demolition of the farm, Schlittenbauer dug in the rubble at the former location of the property because he was looking for his cutting wheel, which he once lent to Andreas Gruber. Schlittenbauer admitted to having told the witness, Hans Yblagger, that the perpetrators first tried to bury the bodies. Schlittenbauer explained that after the judicial commission was there, on the same day in the barn near the location where the bodies were found, he discovered a place where a shovel-deep hole had been dug. The dirt was quite fresh and covered with straw. The witness concluded that the perpetrators wanted to bury the bodies at the time, but the ground was probably too hard.

Schlittenbauer, when asked if he was at home with his wife around the time of the crime, asserted after his second interrogation that he knew very well that he was seen as a perpetrator in the area. He attributed this primarily to his active intervention as a local leader and his willingness to help. For humane reasons he had taken care of everything, but after his experience he had resolved not to "intervene in such a selfless manner" in the future. Police suspicions against Schlittenbauer were not warranted.

Hans and Eduard Schirovsky
Interviewed on 04/05/1922

The statements of the coffee dealers, Hans Schirovsky (born April 15, 1897) and Eduard Schirovsky (born 1904) from Straubing, were recorded on April 5, 1922 in the kitchen of the Hinterkaifeck property. On April 1st, 1922 at noon between 12:00 p.m. and 2:00 p.m. they arrived to take coffee orders. When they entered the property, the witnesses repeatedly knocked on the house windows in the courtyard and shouted for attention, but nobody responded. They then went around the house and looked through the windows in the kitchen and barns. But no person could be seen. Only the dog and cattle could be heard. The dealers discovered that all doors of the property were locked; with the exception of the engine shed gate which was open. Finally, they left the farm and reported their observations to Jakob Sigl and the Schlittenbauer family in Gröbern. The two brothers were unable to provide any suggestions about who might be the perpetrators.

Michael Pöll
Interviewed on 04/05/1922

The witness, Michael Pöll (born 09/27/1865 in Wangen, died 11/08/1924 in Gröbern) was interrogated by Munich police one day after the discovery of the corpses. Pöll testified that Lorenz Schlittenbauer told him that on April 4th, 1922 around
5 p.m. no one was moving about at Hinterkaifeck.

79

Schlittenbauer asked him to go to the farm with Jakob Sigl. At Hinterkaifeck, all the doors were found locked. Only the gate leading to the engine shed was unlocked. On the other side of the engine shed, the southern barn door was blown open and the three people entered the barn. Through the open barn door, a roaming cow peered into the barn.

Pöll stated that Lorenz Schlittenbauer went ahead and entered the barn. Pöll saw him stumble slightly. The witness followed him immediately and searched with his feet on the ground because it was already getting dark. Pöll hit an obstacle with his foot and said to his two companions; "There's something there." Schlittenbauer turned around, first picked up a board and then grabbed a visible human foot. He pulled it out further and recognized Andreas Gruber.

Then three more corpses were seen lying under the hay. Cecilia (Cilli) Gabriel was lying against the wall next to the barn door. Schlittenbauer took the girl and laid her backwards against the forage cutting machine in the barn. The witness and Sigl then left the barn in the direction of the courtyard outside.

Meanwhile, Schlittenbauer had advanced through the barn into the residential wing of the property and opened the front door on the east side from the inside, whereupon the two companions entered. Together they found Joseph Gruber's body in the stroller in the bedroom. From there they went through the kitchen into the maid's room. There was a blanket on the floor with two shoes exposed. Schlittenbauer pushed aside the blanket under which a "strange woman" lay murdered.

According to Pöll, the Gabriel/Gruber family were hardworking, thrifty people who lived very withdrawn from others. The Hinterkaifeckers were generally known to be wealthy. The village also knew that Andreas Gruber had had a sexual relationship with his daughter, Victoria Gabriel. Pöll reported that Lorenz Schlittenbauer intended to marry Victoria Gabriel, but marriage was prevented by Andreas Gruber. The witness was not aware of any recently hostile relationship between Gruber and Schlittenbauer.

Pöll stated that he noticed the silence at Hinterkaifeck on April 1st and April 3rd when he was working in the field. In particular, "the farm dog no longer roamed about", who Pöll described as usually extremely vigilant. On the day of discovery on April 4, 1922 the farm dog was locked in the barn.

Kreszenz Rieger
Interviewed on 04/24/1922 and 07/09/1952)

The farm maid, Kreszenz Rieger (Born April 23, 1897 Oberhausen near Augsburg), who later married a man named Schmidt, was first questioned in April 1922. She claimed to have been employed at Hinterkaifeck from November 1920 until the oat harvest at the end of August to the beginning of September 1921. Detectives found Rieger based on the health insurance receipts for the months of July and August 1921 that were stored on the property from 1921.

Rieger stated that at the time she had a love affair with the unmarried day laborer, Jakob Weber

(Born July 5th, 1887 Karlskron, died May 1921 Munich) and that she was pregnant by Weber. Rieger gave birth to a girl on March 27th at Hinterkaifeck. A short time later on orders of Schrobenhausen physician Dr. Gessner, the baby was placed with a foster family in Rettenbach near Schrobenhausen due to lack of care.

Shortly after Rieger took the job at Hinterkaifeck, the factory worker, Anton Bichler, from Waidhofen made "sexual advances" to her. As she admitted, Bichler had already knocked several times on her bedroom window during the first few days. Rieger could not hear the knocking at the time because she slept in the residential area after the birth. She was later able to see that Bichler's statements were correct from the footprints in the flower beds in front of her window. After the delivery, Bichler also visited her and then came to her bedroom window a few more times. But Rieger never let him in because she was not ready to enter into a relationship with Bichler and to have sexual relations with him. According to Rieger, the farm dog, who was otherwise very vicious, did not bark when Bichler came to her window. Interesting since the dog had even bitten little Cilli in the past.

The witness stated that the Gabriel/Gruber family advised her not to have a relationship with Anton Bichler, because Bichler was a thief. They suspected Bichler had stolen chickens. At that time, Bichler had come to Hinterkaifeck regularly about every fourteen days to three weeks. He also helped with the potato harvest and steam threshing. On one of these occasions, Anton Bichler complained to Rieger about the poor food at Hinterkaifeck. Bichler also knew that the Hinterkaifeck residents had money.

A report by Detective Commissioner George Neuss from the Munich police department to Schrobenhausen police on May 2, 1922, indicated that detectives learned of her through information from the local health insurance fund in Schrobenhausen. Kreszenz Rieger was employed at Hinterkaifeck from October 9, 1921 to February 2, 1922. The period of time deviating from the information provided by the witness was obviously due to the fact that the employer did not register for social security until afterwards. Kreszenz Rieger was not registered for social security for the first few months of her employment at Hinterkaifeck.

After Rieger did not respond to Bichler's multiple requests for dates, she found out from residents of Gröbern that Bichler went around saying that he would have her sooner or later. According to the witness, Victoria Gabriel heard while going to church in Waidhofen that Anton Bichler had stated that the Gabriel/Gruber family was to blame for the fact that he did not seduce Zenzi (Rieger's nickname). According to a resident from Gröbern, whose name Rieger did not know, Bichler was said to have remarked that "the Kaifeckers should all be killed". Rieger claimed to have quit the job at Hinterkaifeck for fear of threats from Anton Bichler, whom she thought was a violent person.

The servant, George Siegl, was supposed to have made a statement similar to Anton Bichler, as Rieger claimed to have learned from another woman whose name she did not know. Rieger also reported by hearsay, that Siegl was said to have stolen smoked meat, eggs, bread and children's clothing at Hinterkaifeck about eight days before starting work. Despite the incident, Victoria put Siegl back into service after Rieger left. However, Siegl ran away after two days, which the witness found out when she picked up her things. Her first thought when she heard about the Hinterkaifeck murders was that Anton Bichler and his brother, Karl, who, in her opinion, stolen a harness in Koppenbach in 1919, along with George Siegl, could have had something to do with the crime. She was mistaken about the Bichler brothers stealing the harness. It was Lorenz and Adam Thaler.

Rieger reported an incident at Hinterkaifeck, in which an unknown man knocked on her window one night. The man turned out to be a farm hand from Gröbern, Joseph Schrittenlocher, who asked if she wanted to let him in. However, it was not a Schrittenlocher that she knew. When Rieger did not let the stranger into her room, whom she only saw from the side in the semi-darkness, the man asked her whether young Victoria would be with old Gruber. When Rieger stated that she did not know, the stranger left again.

Rieger stated that Andreas Gruber and Victoria Gabriel were surprised by her once in the spring of 1921 between 7:00 p.m. and 8:00 p.m. in the barn when she went out to get milk. Rieger saw Victoria laying in the hay with her father on top of her. Victoria Gabriel later said to the witness that she would not have gone out with her father if she had known that Rieger was going to the barn. Shortly after the incident, the witness claimed to have heard when she was interrogated in July 1952, that Andreas Gruber had told Victoria Gabriel that she did not need to marry because as long as he lived, he was there for "this" which obviously meant that he would always satisfy his daughter sexually.

In April 1922, Rieger stated that she knew Lorenz Schlittenbauer, who was said to be the father of the murdered, Joseph Gruber. As long as she was on duty in Hinterkaifeck, he never came to the farm. Old Gruber and Schlittenbauer had spoken to each other, but the women did not talk to Schlittenbauer, as the witness stated. When she was interrogated in July 1952, Rieger reported by hearsay that a married man from Gröbern allegedly had sexual intercourse with Victoria Gabriel when she was already pregnant. Victoria wanted to establish that the man, whose name the witness no longer remembered, was the child's father, and the man was said to have responded when Victoria asked him for something, that he would testify that she was already pregnant when they had sex and that Andreas Gruber, as the father of a child, would come into question. As a result, the Gabriel/Gruber family failed to take action against the man.

Rieger stated that the Hinterkaifeckers were generally unpopular because of their stinginess and that nobody liked them. The witness cannot name specific persons who would have been hostile to the Hinterkaifeckers.

George Siegl
Interviewed on 04/27/1922 and 07/05/1923)

The unmarried servant, George Siegl, (Born March 22nd, 1902 Gröbern) was questioned by police at the end of April 1922 after suspicions expressed by the former Hinterkaifeck maid, Kreszenz Rieger. Siegl claimed to have personally known the Gruber/Gabriel family and to have worked on Hinterkaifeck farm several times during the harvest season for a total of 12 weeks, which he added in a second questioning on July 5, 1923 before the Schrobenhausen District Court. Siegl denied accusations of the maid, Kreszenz Rieger pointing out that there was a mix-up with the 15-year-old, former barn boy at Hinterkaifeck, Joseph Hartl. He was the one who had committed the "breaking and entry theft" at Hinterkaifeck and stole children's clothing in addition to meat and other groceries. Andreas Gruber and Victoria Gabriel told him this. It was generally known that the residents of Hinterkaifeck had money, including gold coins.

The family's farm dog was extremely vigilant. The witness cannot recall that the dog did not "bark" at certain people. Siegl stated that from March 31 to April 1, 1922, he stayed in his room with his employer in Hohenried, the innkeeper Johann Huber. The information was confirmed by the employer.

Michael Bichler
Interviewed on 04/26/1922

The statement of the single butcher, Michael Bichler (Born 09/04/1900 Gröbern) was taken on April

26, 1922 by the Munich detectives. Michael Bichler stated that he knew the murdered people because, according to his own admission, during the time when he was still living with his parents in Gröbern, he helped out several times with farm work on Hinterkaifeck. Michael could name other harvest helpers from this time: Anton Bichler (Waidhofen), Joseph Schrittenlocher, Joseph Schratzebarner and George Siegl who were all from Gröbern. He also knew Kreszenz Rieger, the maid who was working on the farm at the time. Her lover was Anton Bichler from Waidhofen.

Michael indicated Anton Bichler's willingness to use violence to solve problems. The latter had told the witness that he wanted to go to Hinterkaifeck and "knock a few out" for the maid, Kreszenz Rieger, because she had wrongly claimed that Anton had her sexually eight days before the birth of her child on 03/27/1921. The witness was also present when Anton Bichler was asked about the financial assets of the Hinterkaifeckers. Rieger stated, however, according to her own admission, she could not raise any further suspicions against Anton Bichler.

Michael Bichler added, however, that the aforementioned brother, Karl Bichler, tried to persuade him to steal gold coins from the Gabriel/Gruber family. When the witness refused, Karl Bichler turned to other possible crimes such as cattle and bicycle theft from a landlord in Waidhofen and the theft of 8,000 marks from Joseph Bichler, one of Karl Bichler's four brothers. Karl Bichler also inquired about the possibility of stealing two fresh sacks of stolen tobacco leaves and asked Michael whether he knew "where to get potatoes from the cart". As the witness claimed to have found out from third parties, Karl Bichler was said to have stolen sheep in Koppenbach which was near Waidhofen. The witness also reported from hearsay that Karl Bichler had announced that he no longer wanted to work, "and if he had to, he would get his hands of blood". The phrase "get your hands full of blood" is probably just another form of "get your hands dirty".

In conclusion, Michael stated that he had already reported this to the Schrobenhausen police on April 12, 1922 and the other statements made to him by third parties. He was told there that Karl Bichler was cleared as the perpetrator, as he could prove his alibi during the critical period. The officer in question referred Michael to the Hohenwart police station, which was now responsible for the case.

Anton Bichler
Interviewed on 05/04/1922

The unmarried Swiss milker, Anton Bichler, (Born April 12th, 1891 Augsburg-Pfersee) was interrogated by Munich detectives on May 4th, 1922, based on incriminating information from the former maid at Hinterkaifeck, Kreszenz Rieger, and the butcher, Michael Bichler. Bichler stated that he had worked for various employers since mid-July 1920. The witness had been employed as a Swiss citizen at Gut Lindahof in the Althegnenberg community in the Fürstenfeldbruck district since February 6, 1922. Althegnenberg is about 53 kilometers from Gröbern.

Anton Bichler stated that he wanted to have a love affair with Kreszenz Rieger, who worked as a maid at Hinterkaifeck in 1920 and 1921. This was why he had come to the maid's bedroom window several times at night in Hinterkaifeck. Rieger only let him into her room once. He broke off the relationship when he met Rieger accompanied by a man in the Schrobenhausen Inn Grieser. Bichler denied that he ever threatened Kreszenz Rieger or made threats against the Gabriel/Gruber family. The witness admitted that he occasionally expressed displeasure about the on-site food service when he helped with steam threshing on the farm. Contrary to the information provided by Rieger, the farm dog lunged when Bichler entered the farm.

The murder victims were known to him personally. They were thrifty, hardworking and very withdrawn people who avoided all interaction with other people. Bichler could not provide information about people who have been employed on the property beyond those already known. Anton admitted in 1921 to poaching for ravens in the hunting district of the lawyer, Anton Schneider, from Schrobenhausen in the Wangen district. He had used an infantry rifle from the army. After being reprimanded by the hunting tenant, he stopped going to the hunting area. He had not been in Waidhofen since May 4, 1921.

Regarding the relationship to his brother, Karl Bichler, who until recently also worked on the Lindahof estate, there could be no question of brotherly hostility. For the time of the crime, Anton Bichler stated that from March 31 to April 1st, 1922, he and his brother Karl stayed at Gut Lindahof and did not leave the municipality of Althegnenberg. They had spent the evening of March 31, 1922 in the Bergmüller inn in Althegnenberg, which could be confirmed by three named witnesses. One of the witnesses, the commercial builder and foreman at Gut Lindahof, Michael Huber, confirmed Bichler's statements during his interrogation on site on the same day which included information about a strained relationship between the brothers.

Karl Bichler
Interviewed on 04/05/1922

The unmarried laborer, Karl Bichler, (Born October 12, 1901 Waidhofen) was taken into custody on May 4, 1922 and interrogated on site in Althegnenberg. The arrest was preceded by testimony according to which Karl Bichler supposedly made assumptions about gold money at Hinterkaifeck prior to the murder and attempted to induce witnesses to break into Hinterkaifeck together. In a report from Detective George Neuss to the Munich Police Department dated May 2, 1922, Karl Bichler was described as suspected of murder in numerous relevant investigations.

"As can be seen from the findings so far, he is portrayed as a work-shy person who is very inclined to property crimes. According to information provided by Simon Schönecker, he became annoyed by the working residents in Waidhofen in the summer of 1921 and drifted around the area, until the application for moving into a workhouse was received by the Waidhofen municipal administration. At a meeting at

the Reiger Inn in Waidhofen Karl Bichler talked to
Schönecker, who had asked him how he could avoid
work, and uttered: 'Yes, Simmerl, I don't work
anymore, I'm not so stupid that I get my hands dirty, so
it goes to getting my hands bloody.

During his interrogation, Karl Bichler confirmed
the short-term employment relationships since July
1921 and stated that he accepted a position as a servant
at Gut Lindahof on March 2 or 3, 1922.

He had known the murdered people in
Hinterkaifeck personally except for the maidservant -
because he had been working on site as a potato picker
in autumn 1919. He was aware of the financial
circumstances of the Gabriel/Gruber family insofar as
he learned from conversations with farms hands that
the people paying them were wealthy and also had gold
money. Karl Bichler, on the other hand, denied ever
having tried to persuade third parties to rob the family
or nor did he state that Andreas Gruber must be "taken
care of." The witness insisted that he only said that no
one would have to work if they had money like the
Grubers. The accusations made by Michael Bichler,
prompting the arrest of Karl Bichler were false.

This also applied to the claim that Bichler
remarked that he no longer wanted to work, even if he
had to get his hands bloody. Rather, he told third parties
that he no longer wanted to get his hands dirty, which,
according to the person questioned, related to his
activity digging potatoes.

The Karl admitted that he was interested in a
narcotic that could be used to paralyze a dog. The
reason for wanting the narcotic was unclear, with the

witness asserting that he had not possessed any such drug to date. Bichler admitted that from 1914 to February 1922, around a dozen offenses could be attributed to property crime and stolen goods, which mainly related to small livestock, little amounts of money and agricultural products. It seemed that Karl had quite a rap sheet with not all crimes being relevant to the Hinterkaifeck crimes.

The criminal history of the suspect included obtaining and fencing stolen property along with minor property crimes characterized as nonviolent. Karl Bichler would have avoided physical confrontation with the crime victims if he had planned to steal the family's gold money. Whoever planned the crime of stealing the Gruber gold appeared to be waiting for at a time when all or most of the family members were working outside the residential wing as indicated by the moved tiles on the roof.

Jakob Sigl
Interviewed 04/05/1922 and 01/10/1952)

The farmer Jakob Sigl (Born July 17, 1891 Gröbern, died 1971) was summoned by Munich detectives for the first time as one of three witnesses on April 5th, 1922. A second, more extensive questioning was conducted on the murders in early 1952. Sigl lived in Gröbern until 1933, after that in the community of Schiitberg in the district of Aichach some 19 kilometers away.

Sigl testified that Lorenz Schlittenbauer went to his house at No. 27 Gröbern on April 4, 1922 around 5:00 p.m. saying that something was wrong with the

Grubers. Either they were "busy" or something else was going on. Schlittenbauer had also mentioned that the mechanic had been there fixing an engine.

Schlittenbauer asked Sigl to go to Hinterkaifeck with him along with the neighboring farmer, Pöll. Schlittenbauer also took his 16-year-old son, Johann Schlittenbauer, with them.

When they arrived at the property, they found all the doors locked, with exception of the door to the engine shed. In the second interrogation, Sigl added that they did not go to any front door or window, but instead went directly to the barn door at the behest of Schlittenbauer. The barn door was opened by force. Here Schlittenbauer told the witness to help him pull the gate open. When entering the barn, an untied cow looked through the barn door into the barn. Schlittenbauer went ahead into the barn, followed by Sigl and Pöll, and climbed over a "board" to tie up the cow. The witness followed him and hit something with his foot. Then Pöll said: "That's him, that's Gruber." Sigl shouted, "Lenz something is over there!" Schlittenbauer turned around, grabbed the foot and pulled it out and picked up the board, which was covered with hay. Finally, they could see four corpses lying on the floor.

Sigl stated that Schlittenbauer now repositioned all four corpses one after the other north toward the threshing room. When he and Pöll asked him to leave the corpses as they were, Schlittenbauer replied that he had to see everything carefully. The witness could not provide any information about the types of injuries. He could only state that all four corpses had their faces covered with blood and that the girl (meaning, Cilli) was holding hair in her hands.

Schlittenbauer implored, "Where is my little boy?" and went through the barn into the interior of the house, while the Sigl and Pöll left the barn heading to the courtyard. Schlittenbauer then opened the front door from the inside. Here the witness, who had been waiting in the courtyard, could hear Schlittenbauer turn the door lock with a key.

Immediately after entering the hall, Sigl wanted to open the door to the bedroom, which he only accomplished after Schlittenbauer told him that he had to lift the handle to open it. In the bedroom, the 2 year-old Joseph Gruber, lay dead in his stroller (the age of the child has been stated from eighteen months to twenty-four months in reports). Pieces of the child's brain stuck to the destroyed roof of the stroller. The doors of the cabinets in the bedroom had been open, but nothing was out of order. Schlittenbauer looked for a candle and lit it as a memorial for "his boy".

From the bedroom Sigl went into the kitchen. On the kitchen stove there was a full enamel bowl with bread soup, from which nothing had been dished up. From the kitchen in the adjoining maid's room, he could see a blanket lying on the floor from which two shoes peeked out. Schlittenbauer pulled the covers off, revealing a female corpse. Schlittenbauer immediately announced, "This is a stranger." Sigl claimed to have gone into the bedroom of the Gruber couple afterwards. He hadn't noticed anything there out of place and the bed was still made. Sigl and Pöll then left the house while Schlittenbauer stayed behind and fed the cattle.

In his second interrogation, Sigl added that he went into the barn from the kitchen. The cattle did not give him the impression that they had been neglected for several days. The witness remembered that there was a calf, which would certainly have bellowed loudly if it had not been fed for a long time.

There were also 8-week-old piglets in the barn who behaved quietly. Schlittenbauer went into the cellar of the property, fetched milk and fed the pigs with it. He also asked the witness to go up to the loft and throw down hay to threshing floor, so that the cattle could be fed. However, the witness and Pöll did not comply with the request. Sigl said that they would go home and report the bodies to the police. Schlittenbauer then sent his son, Johann. to the mayor in Wangen. Little by little, people from all over the area arrived at the deserted farm, while Sigl, as he had stated, did not involve himself further.

When Sigl came back to the scene of the crime the next day to describe his perceptions from the on-site visit to the judicial commission, a hay rope hung in the threshing floor near the hay loft area, which was definitely had not there the day before.

Jakob Sigl reported that Lorenz Schlittenbauer had wanted to marry Victoria Gabriel at the time when he thought he was the father of the illegitimate child about 2 years ago. Andreas Gruber, however, prevented the marriage, according to the witness, and threatened that he would leave the house if the marriage took place, (So why would two abused women care if Andreas left the house? Victoria, who owned the farm, appeared perfectly able to run the business). Recently, however, Gruber had no longer been hostile to Schlittenbauer. Sigl later added that he heard from stories that Andreas Gruber had committed incest with his biological daughter, Victoria. Presumably also at the time when Victoria was already with Cilli.

Victoria was married to Karl Gabriel at the time which was why he temporarily returned to his parents' house in Laag shortly after the wedding. After the death of his first wife, Lorenz Schlittenbauer had an intimate relationship with Victoria. When she was pregnant, Schlittenbauer told the witness that he was not the father of the expected child, but Andreas Gruber. Victoria Gabriel admitted this to Schlittenbauer.

Schlittenbauer then filed a complaint of incest against Gruber. The witness reported from hearsay that Victoria Gabriel had petitioned Lorenz Schlittenbauer to withdraw the charge, whereupon Andreas Gruber was released from custody. As Sigl stated, Schlittenbauer was said to have subsequently recognized paternity, but did not pay any child support. For this reason, Victoria Gabriel went to the Schrobenhausen District Court in the second half of March 1922 to bring claims against Schlittenbauer. After Sigl, Gabriel was accompanied by the Gröbern innkeeper, Thomas Schwaiger. On the way to Schrobenhausen, Victoria Gabriel was said to have told Schwaiger about her plan.

The Hinterkaifeck family were very thrifty and hardworking people and, as Sigl suspected, also quite wealthy. In 1952, Sigl stated that he had been to the cattle market in Schrobenhausen on the Thursday before the crime. There his father-in-law, Kaspar

Stegmeier, told him that that day he passed the Hinterkaifeck estate on the way to Schrobenhausen. There Stegmeier had a conversation with Andreas Gruber. Gruber said that there was a trail in the snow leading to his property and that he believed rascals were in his house. Stegmeier advised Gruber to have the property searched by the police, whereupon the Gruber replied that he was not afraid.

As the witness noted, the farm dog on Hinterkaifeck was an aggressive watchdog. He was locked in the barn every evening, where he still was on April 4, 1922 when the witnesses penetrated through the barn door.

Albert Hofner
Interviewed on 05/15/1925

The operations manager of a machine factory in Reichertshausen, near Pfaffenhofen, Albert Hofner (born October 1, 1902 Königsfeld near Pfaffenhofen), was questioned by Munich detectives for the first time more than three years after the crime.

The retired police commander from Schwarzenbach am Wald, who took his testimony, stated in a letter to the Neuburg Public Prosecutor that the mechanic may have committed the robbery and murders. During processing of the testimony, which was no longer being pursued due to incorrect assumptions made by police about circumstances surrounding the crime, it turned out that Albert Hofner had not yet been questioned.

Hofner testified that he was the one who repaired the Sendling 4 HP stationary engine on

Hinterkaifeck before Easter 1922. The witness cannot remember who gave him the repair order back then or what day he rode his motorbike to Hinterkaifeck; but it must have been a Monday or Tuesday, because the bad weather the week before meant that he had to postpone the repairs to the beginning of the coming week. He left Pfaffenhofen around 7:00 am. Due to the poor road conditions, it took him a little longer to get to Hinterkaifeck some 18 km away. During his drive through Wangen, he met Mayor Gregers and had a chat with him. Hofner informed the mayor that he was on his way to Hinterkaifeck to repair the engine.

Coming from Gröbern, Hofner first tried to push his bike, which had a tool bag on it, through a gate of the wooden fence on the north side of the property. Since the door was locked, Hofner returned to the field path and used a gap in the fence near the bakery to access the rear of the property. Since the back door was also locked, he looked through the kitchen window and one of the barn windows into the building interior; but did not find anyone.

Hofner used the back door despite the gully in front of it because he had been there 1 to 2 years prior, and entered the house through the back door and was greeted in the kitchen by the family. Hofner reported that he heard nothing more than the dog barking and the loud mooing of cows. He was not concerned by nobody being around, as he had often heard that old Gruber was an eccentric and that he often did not come home from the field. the cattle were often left to their own devices during the day.

According to Hofner, he then parked his bike under a fruit tree near the back door and sat on the bike waiting for about an hour. He had tried several times to draw attention to himself by whistling loudly through his fingers, since someone had been working with draft animals in the field nearby and he had assumed that it might be someone from the farm. This could explain why Hofner did not enter house to look for the residents.

Since he had to do other work in the area that day, Hofner went to the engine shed after waiting about an hour at around 10:00 am to examine the lock. Since the door was only secured with a padlock, he pried the hook attached to the door frame off and opened the door. Hofner stated that he immediately started repairs to the engine and installed a new cylinder head gasket. He was finished with the work after about 4.5 hours, around 2:30 p.m. Then he gave the engine a test run. He hoped to make himself noticeable over the engine exhaust noise. To check the engine, he should actually have started the cooling water pump. However, there was no more water in the water pit next to the engine, which Hofner noticed when a screw nut fell into the pit during the repair work. Because Hofner would have had to gain entry into the house, in order to get a drive belt and a bucket, he did not test the cylinder head gasket with water.

When no one appeared despite the engine rumble, Hofner turned it off, locked the engine shed and walked through the vegetable garden on the west side of the main house into the farm courtyard.

The witness stated that the barn door was wide open (So why did Schlittenbauer have to break in?). For reasons of decency, he did not go into the barn, but only looked into it from a distance of about 3 meters.

However, nobody was there. He then went to the front door, which was locked. In front of the door, the farm dog was tied up and barked viciously. Hofner explained that he did not pay any further attention to the dog, as he was used to being barked at by dogs when he entered farms for his job (Hofner did not mention the dog being wounded). He then looked into the windows to the left and right of the front door, but did not see anyone, so he set off on his way to the next job.

On his return trip through Gröbern, shortly after 2:30 p.m., Hofner asked two women working in the garden of the first property to the left of the main street, whom Hofner assumed were maids, if they would tell the Hinterkaifecks that a mechanic from Ptaffenhoten repaired the engine. The women replied that it would make the residents happy.

Then Hofner drove to Kaifeck to the south, about 1.7 km away, to repair another engine. He told the farmer in question, Blasius Lebmeier, that he had not met anyone at Hinterkaifeck. Lebmeier replied that the Grubers often spent the whole day with the children in the forest cutting wood and stayed until evening. Hofner stated that the second repair took about 45 to 60 minutes and that he left for Pfafffenhofen around 5:30 p.m. In Wangen he spoke to Mayor Gregers again and informed him that he was going to repair another engine in Kaifeck. Hofner said he was back in Pfaffenhofen around 7:00 p.m.

In view of the time span between the completion of the work on Hinterkaifeck and Hofner's arrival in Pfaffenhofen, which cannot be explained by repair times and travel times alone, it can be assumed that

Hofner's time in Kaifeck as well as his second visit in Wangen was accurate from midday as he described it in detail. The conversation with the two young women in Gröbern was more than likely only a brief exchange.

Wenzeslaus Bley
Interviewed on 08/08/1930

Information provided by the carpenter, Wenzeslaus Bley (Born 10/16/1884 Waidhofen) who was questioned by Munich detectives on August 8, 1930, was largely based on hearsay. On the day before the murder, Andreas Gruber, according to the witness, said in the Vogel hardware store in Schrobenhausen that he wanted to get home quickly because something was wrong in his house. During the night he heard footsteps in the attic. He looked in the attic with the light on, but couldn't see anything. In the early morning Gruber discovered footprints in the fresh snow that led to the farm from the woods, but not back again.

On Saturday, April 1st, 1922, the carpenter, Michael Plöckl, from Gröbern came by on the way home through Hinterkaifeck at around 11:30 p.m. He saw that a fire had burned in the bakery at the back of the property, at the same time a man closed the opening from which the light had come. and came up to him with a flashlight. The man held the flashlight in front of him with an outstretched arm and shone it directly into Plöckl's face. The stranger then went back to the courtyard without saying a word. Plöckl was afraid and fled as he told Bley.

Bley also described an incident from the year 1924, according to which Lorenz Schlittenbauer made a bold statement in the Schwaiger Tavern about the number of perpetrators and the possible layout of the crime. Schlittenbauer was said to have given a first-person explanation of events in the barn and the emergence of footprints facing the farm in the fresh snow after a remark by the pub owner that the murders were certainly committed by three to four perpetrators. Lorenz stated that he had made the tracks by walking forward, then backward.

When the two people present asked whether he was ultimately the culprit, Schlittenbauer replied that he had only given a description of how the crime could have happened from his point of view. Bley stated that Schlittenbauer was extremely intelligent, had a good grasp of things and that Schlittenbauer suffered from asthma. By hearsay, Bley reported that at the time the murders became known, Anna Schlittenbauer was said to have mentioned to Jakob Sigl that her husband Lorenz Schlittenbauer had been sleeping in the hay for a few days because hay thieves were suspected to be in the area.

Hans Yblagger
Interviewed on 02/19/1931

The witness, Hans Yblagger (Born October 19, 1886, Mosach), was questioned about the murders on February 19, 1931 in the Bad Reichenhall District Court. Yblagger stated that from October 1922 to October 1927 he worked as a teacher, at the Waidhofen elementary school, in which Gröbern and

Hinterkaifeck belonged. The witness described a meeting with Lorenz Schlittenbauer in April or May 1925 at the former location of the Hinterkaifeck farm. At that time the witness went to the property on foot together with his father-in-law, Joseph Müller, from Munich, who had been visiting and wanted to see the murder scene. At that time the house was almost completely demolished. Only the foundation walls were still standing, and the entrance to the basement in the middle had been preserved, with the cellar entrance being open.

When the witness stepped out of the forest with his father-in-law coming from the south-east, which was near the property and through which the footpath from Waidhofen to Hinterkaifeck leads, he saw Lorenz Schlittenbauer in the middle of the property studying the cellar entrance. Schlittenbauer looked down through the cellar opening in a bent posture. He was "completely absorbed in thought" and only noticed the approaching men when they were about 5 to 7 meters away from him.

Schlittenbauer then immediately began to talk without being prompted by the two men and was amazed at the thickness of the cellar walls. He then told them about the murder case without being asked and explained where the individual corpses had been laying. Schlittenbauer led Yblagger to the outermost corner of the barn, which had been the feed room and said that the perpetrator wanted to dig a hole there to bury the corpses. He elaborated that a spot had been found there where the perpetrator had already started the excavation. When Yblagger replied that the perpetrator would then very likely have to come from the local area, as otherwise he would have tried to leave the crime scene as quickly as possible Schlittenbauer vigorously rejected this idea. The witness could not say whether, and to what extent, his father-in-law, who had been walking around the property, overheard the exchange. Yblagger noted that Schlittenbauer was a person whose mood often fluctuated. The witness had not reported the incident at the demolition site to the public prosecutor's office, as he did not consider it to be relevant to the investigation.

Sofie Fuchs
Interviewed on 12/1951

The farmer's widow, Sofie Fuchs (Born December 16, 1915 Gröbern), was interrogated for the first time by Munich detectives in December 1951. The witness stated that she saw her school friend, Cecilia Gabriel, for the last time on March 31, 1922. On that day, Cecilia Gabriel fell asleep during class. As a reason for her fatigue, she told the teacher that her grandfather hit her mother (Victoria Gabriel) the previous night, whereupon the mother ran away. They then went on a search with the lantern and the dog, but could not find her mother and believed that she was dead or had gone to the Paar, a tributary of the Danube.

At dawn, Victoria was found sitting on a tree trunk in the forest. The witness remembered that Cecilia Gabriel was absent from school the next day April 1st, 1922, which was why an Our Father was prayed in class for her speedy recovery. The witness testified that Cecilia was often ill and therefore often stayed home from school.

Michael Plöckl (senior)
Interviewed 12/1951

Michael Plöckl (senior) (Born October 26th, 1870 in Eulenried) a Gröbern contractor, formerly from the Schrobenhausen district, testified when he was interrogated in December 1951 that he helped to demolish the Hinterkaifeck farm in February 1923. The witness was the father of Michael Plöckl, who claimed to have seen smoke in the oven in Hinterkaifeck and a person with a flashlight at the beginning of April 1922, could remember that Joseph Gabriel from Laag showed him the pickaxe at the time, which was found during demolition work under the rafters, and immediately after their discovery. The tool was a mattock that was attached to the handle with screws. There was still blood on the pick, which the witness merely looked at but not touched.

George Kerner
Interviewed on 11/27/1951

The married butcher, George Kerner (Born March 5, 1907 Schrobenhausen) was questioned by police at the end of November 1951.

After his father's death in World War I, his mother moved from Augsburg to Schrobenhausen, where George Kerner grew up with his half-brother Matthäus Eser in the grandfather's house. The witness was thus already familiar with the Hinterkaifeck farmhouse from the time before the crime. As Kerner reported, at the age of 13 or 14 he came to the farm with his brother collecting mushrooms or firewood in the surrounding woods and asked for something to eat or milk. The witness can remember having been in the kitchen several times. From memory, Kerner drew a hand sketch of the room layout on Hinterkaifeck.

George Kerner testified that the Hinterkaifeckers were generally known as "stingy people"; however, they would never have asked him for something in return.

After the murders became known, Kerner went to the crime scene to watch the investigation. There, according to Kerner, he also saw the six corpses. Four corpses had already been lying "outside on the threshing floor"; the maid was lying in her room, fully dressed, and the slain child was in the stroller. The witness could allegedly remember numerous details when questioned about the murders years later.

The witness stated that the coroner ate smoked meat in the property's kitchen.

Cilli Gabriel was injured in her jaw and held a tuft of female hair in her hand. The witness assumed that this was her own hair, which she tore out in pain and agony. There were bloody finger strokes on Cecilia Gabriel's neck. It was Kerner's opinion it was another a sign that the girl had moved her hand over the painful wound on her chin.

Andreas Gruber was seriously injured on the left side. Kerner claimed that in his "youthful curiosity" he looked at the place in the hayloft above the barn where the perpetrator or perpetrators would probably have been. He could remember that near the hay indentions there were rinds of bacon and fat residues from smoked food, from which he concluded that someone must have either lived for a long time in or frequently sought shelter. In the vicinity of the hay piles, roof tiles had apparently been pushed aside so that the perpetrator could have an overview of everything.

In addition, a hay rope was fastened in the middle of the crossbeam, where someone could lower themselves quickly as possible onto the threshing floor if necessary. According to the witness, the rope did not hang down all the time, but was temporarily pulled up by the perpetrators so that no one would notice.

It is most likely that Kerner's recollections were a combination of personal memories police reports and autopsy conclusions just a few days after the discovery and events almost 30 years after the fact. Pictures of the corpses were printed in the daily newspapers where he could have gotten that information. His sketch was not very detailed. His "memories" were probably embellished by years of media reports and public talk.

Kerner's observations in the kitchen may relate to April 5, 1922 when Kerner visited the crime scene on that day. On the same day that the coroner, District Court Doctor Dr. Johann Baptist Aumüller, was present at the crime scene. The autopsies were conducted on April 6 and 7, 1922 and it cannot be assumed that Aumüller was in the farm kitchen at the same time as Kerner.

Regarding the mistakes Kerner made with some details, it is also questionable whether and to what extent the consumption of smoked meat in the kitchen can be attributed to the coroner or other officials, especially since on April 5th in addition to up to 20 investigators, other people had been on the property. According to relevant documents, several people had been associated with the removal and consumption of smoked meat. Schlittenbauer also had encouraged people to eat food at the crime scene.

Andreas Schwaiger
Interviewed on 12/17/1951 and 04/07/1980

The farmer and innkeeper, Andreas Schwaiger (Born 02/12/1897 Gröbern, died 1984) was first arrested in December 1951 in the Hinterkaifeck murder case. A second interrogation took place at the beginning of the 1980s by Ingolstadt police detectives.

Schwaiger claimed to have lived in Gröbern since birth and to have known the Gabriel/Gruber family well. He often came to Hinterkaifeck and helped out with the threshing, which was why he was familiar with the property. The Grubers bought beer from him. Andreas Gruber was a helpful person, but on the other hand, also very aloof. He didn't confide in everyone about his private affairs.

On Tuesday, April 4, 1922, when Schwaiger was busy on his property, Lorenz Schlittenbauer's children came by around 4:00 p.m. and reported that everyone in Hinterkaifeck had been beaten. The witness then interrupted his work and went to Hinterkaifeck along with his mother, Franziska Schwaiger and his maid at the time. There he met the farmers from Gröbern, Schlittenbauer, Pöll and Sigl, who told him that all residents were dead. Then the four men went into the barn. The barn was entered through the gate that was next to the engine shed. The corpses of Andreas Gruber, Cecilia Gruber and Victoria Gabriel were in the barn in front of the door that led from the barn into the feed room. According to the witness, the corpses had already been laid next to the wall by Schlittenbauer and Pöll to gain access to the barn.

The body of 7-year-old Cecilia Gabriel was lying in the feeding room, whereby the witness initially had the impression that the girl's throat had been cut and she was then killed with a blow to the right half of the face near the nose. A 2-year-old cow was grazing in the barn. When the witness went on through to the barn, he saw a pickaxe lying in the feed room, which the animals had licked. According to the witness, the barn was in good order as it had been set up the prior evening. The manure had not been cleared away. Schwaiger had the impression that the cattle were "quietly perishing." He said that if the cattle were not given anything to eat for three to four days, they would begin to rest and sleep. According to Schwaiger, it was possible that the calves also had not been fed for several days. He recalled two calves with the appearance of pending death. The large animals in the barn had hunched backs, which was an indication of dehydration.

The bread soup was still on the stove in the kitchen. In the adjoining maid's room, the dead maid was lying on the floor under the bed. The maid had injuries on the right side of her face. Blood had leaked from the dead woman's nose and mouth, and she lay in a puddle of dried blood. A rucksack, packed and ready for travel was on ledge below the bedroom window. According to Schwaiger, it appeared that the maid had heard a noise and had wanted to leave the house.

In Victoria Gabriel's bedroom there was a stroller that was covered with a dark hood. After removing the cover, it was clear that a blow had been struck through the stroller hood, which fatally struck the child lying inside. Schwaiger stated that the blow was struck with the cutting edge, and with such force that the child's brain splattered the stroller cover underneath and the bedroom floor.

The beds in the room had not been used. Only on the back bed there were could see impressions at the head end, which indicated that someone must have been sitting on the edge of the bed. An open wallet was lying on the pillow. On the left wall of the bedroom there were three clothes cabinets that were only opened after the public prosecutor's office had arrived. The witness recalled that gold money was found in a clothes locker on the right side. The money was in a tin can that was covered with white towels.

Schwaiger claimed that after the bodies were found, he went to the Gabriel family in Laag less than a mile away and reported the murders. Then he went to Pastor Haas in Waidhofen approximately one mile south, but they didn't believe him there. He then went to the postman, Konrad Mehl, in Waidhofen and asked that the public prosecutor and criminal police in Munich be notified. When the witness returned to Hinterkaifeck some two miles away numerous people were already there. The witness had not been assigned to guard it that evening.

In the residential section of the Hinterkaifeck property, stairs could be used to get to the attic/hay loft where the grain, flour, etc. were stored. There was no firewall there. According to the information provided by Schwaiger, the detectives made several farm sketches in 1951/1952, including a view of the front and back of the Hinterkaifeck.

Hay was stored above the barn, which could be thrown in through to the loft. There was a ladder in the barn where one could get to the hayloft. Schwaiger could no longer say where exactly the ladder was. The witness thought he recalled a hay rope was hanging on the crossbeam in the barn. A dog was also kept on Hinterkaifeck. The dog was found in the barn when the crime was discovered and constantly tilted his head to the side because his head was injured.

The witness stated that his father, Thomas Schwaiger, and his brother told him that on Thursday, when the market was in Schrobenhausen, that Andreas Gruber was standing behind the property at the well. When Thomas Schwaiger greeted Gruber as he drove by, he said that there were footprints on his property, but no longer visible when they talked. The footprints could be clearly seen then because it was snowing slightly at that time. Thomas Schwaiger replied that it was now the end of March and that the rains would come. This was delayed so the footprints remained visible in the ground.

In July 1980, Andreas Schwaiger stated that the mattock, which the police identified as the murder weapon, did not belong to Andreas Gruber, but to Lorenz Schlittenbauer. Schlittenbauer wanted the mattock back, which Gruber had allegedly stolen from him, shortly after it was found in 1923, but did not get it because it had been confiscated by Munich police.

Johann Freundl
Interviewed on 12/17/1951

The forest ranger, Johann Freundl (Born 07/03/1882 Gröbern) was interrogated on December 17, 1951 by officers of the Baden State Police regarding the Hinterkaifeck murders. He had helped out at Hinterkaifeck as a handyman on the farm and did threshing work. In his opinion, the Hintererkaifecks were economically well situated.

The witness reported that he heard about the murders at Hinterkaifeck from Kaspar Stegmeier, who was next door to the farm on the day of the incident at around 5:00 p.m. They went together across country, through meadows and fields to the property. On the way there, they were met by farmers Jakob Sigl and Michael Pöll, who were on the way home. They informed them that all residents of Hinterkaifeck had been slain. Freundl also reported that when he arrived, only the "farmers and town leader", Lorenz Schlittenbauer were on the property.

Allegedly the two men entered the property through the front door, but Freundl could no longer remember exactly where they met Schlittenbauer. Schlittenbauer showed the two men the dead in the barn where an old barn door and some hay was placed on the corpses. Then he led the two of them into the maid's room. Maria Baumgartner's body was lying there on the floor. Then Schlittenbauer went to Victoria Gabriel's bedroom and showed them the body

112

of the little boy in the stroller. Schlittenbauer pointed out an empty wallet lying on Victoria Gabriel's bed in the middle of the blanket.

Little by little, more people came to the farm then finally Mayor Gregers and the Hohenwart police.

The farm dog was in the barn; the cattle had behaved quietly because they had been looked after by Schlittenbauer since the discovery. The witness was of the opinion that the three calves in the barn in particular would have made a loud noise if they had not been fed for a long time. Freundl reported that there was a tub of meat (Pokeflejsch) in the engine shed and that Schlittenbauer told him to help himself. The witness had noticed that Schlittenbauer had made no attempt to stop curious people at the crime scene. Freundl said that he even asked the mayor to do something about the destruction of evidence. Schlittenbauer replied that the people were already there and that there was nothing more he could do.

Freundl claimed to have been assigned to guard the farm several times in the following period. There were always three people on the night watch. The last time Freundl came into contact with the residents of Hinterkaifeck was when he helped to carry the coffins of the six victims to the Waidhofen cemetery on the day of the funeral (April 8, 1922).

Joseph Schrittenlocher
Interviewed on 12/17/1951 and 07/01/1952

The farmer, Joseph Schrittenlocher (Born 09/30/1896 Gröbern), resident of Gröbern, was questioned in December 1951 and in July 1952 by Munich detectives. The witness stated that he grew up in Gröbern and that he came to Hinterkaifeck often when he was very young.

Schrittenlocher testified that at the beginning of April 1922, when he returned home from shopping for geese at around 4 p.m., he heard from villagers that the people behind the quarry had been slain. Then he went to Hinterkaifeck. When he arrived, there were already some people in the courtyard. The witness remembered that the farmers, Lorenz Schlittenbauer and Jakob Sigl were among those present.

At first, they did not dare to go onto the property. Schrittenlocher could longer say through which door one could get into the building. The slain Andreas Gruber, his wife, his daughter and Cecilia Gabriel were lying in the barn behind the door. When he went through the barn into the living area, Schrittenlocher didn't notice anything unusual. The dog who stayed back was in the house and also seemed to have been hit because his head was injured. Schrittenlocher had reached Victoria Gabriel's bedroom through the kitchen. There was a stroller in front of the bed, the roof of which was broken. When the witness looked into the stroller, he could see that the child had been killed by a violent blow to the head. Splinters of the head and parts of the brain were on the stroller hood. According to the witness, the blow must

114

have been made with the broad side of the mattock. The witness could not provide any precise details about the maid's body. He recalled that the maid was fully clothed. There was a full rucksack on the windowsill in the maid's room, which obviously hadn't been unpacked yet.

In the course of time, more and more people came to the property, while Schrittenlocher left the residential wing with the images of what he had seen and sat in the tool shed. Schrittenlocher said that he had to keep watch on the property.

According to Schrittenlocher, it was possible to get to the attic from the threshing floor. The witness cannot say whether there was a ladder near the feed room. Although he often worked for Gruber, he was never in the attic. The witness also could not recall whether a hay rope was hanging in the barn.

Andreas Gruber was a man who helped everyone out. If you worked for him, he paid well, but the food was less commendable. Cecilia Gruber ran the household. Andreas Gruber and Victoria Gabriel did the field work and all other agricultural work. Andreas Gruber never talked about family problems. In this regard he was very private, as Schrittenlocher testified at the end of 1951.

At the second interrogation in July 1952, Schrittenlocher stated that he had heard from hearsay that Andreas Gruber had a "incestual relationship" with his daughter, Victoria Gabriel. Schrittenlocher was even present when Gruber was arrested by police for the relationship with his daughter. In addition to Schrittenlocher, the farmers, Schrätzbarner and Kreitmeier from Gröbern, were on site doing threshing one time. When the three men were standing together by the steam threshing machine, which was still used to do the threshing at the time, Andreas Gruber came along. One of the men greeted Gruber with the words: "Good morning, old man you up already?" He replied that he almost never went to bed last night. When Kreitmeier asked him whether he had worked too hard, Gruber replied that his daughter Victoria had given birth last night, which was July 7, 1919.

In response to the remark that this was not so bad after all, Gruber said: "Yes, from my point of view it should have been someone else waiting for it. From Gruber's answer it was concluded that he did not agree with who the father of the child was, but without naming the actual father or making any indications as to who was the father of the child. In general, it was said that Andreas Gruber could be considered the father of Joseph Gruber. In this context, Schrittenlocher described the incident that happened when he did thresh work on Hinterkaifeck one autumn day in 1919.

On the day the bodies were found the witness was either in the kitchen or bedroom, he could not be sure. The farm dog was injured in the head and Schrittenlocher assumed as the dog's eye was knocked out.

The witness stated that on the night of April 2nd to 3rd, 1922, he was assigned to Hinterkaifeck together with two other farmers from Gröbern as a guard. Schrätzbarner started work at midnight. Most of the night the three men stayed in the bakery at the back of the property. A fire was made in the oven to warm up, and the logs that were already in the oven were burned, which, as the witness suspected, were placed there by the victims. During the night watch, which lasted until dawn, the three men walked across the courtyard every now and then without entering the premises of the property.

Schrätzbarner stated that the property was fenced in, with the wooden fence poles already quite rotten. The engine shed was added to the road side of the house. It was brick that was firmly connected to the main building. One could enter the road side through a door installed there, but could not enter the barn or the house.

The house had two front doors. In order to be able to use the rear door of the property, the gutter in front of it had to be pushed aside. A staircase led to the attic from the hallway. Here one came first to the grain storage. From there one could continue up to the loft (although the witness can no longer say how exactly one got there). Around 15 to 20 pieces of smoked meat were hanging in the smokehouse near the fireplace in the attic at the time of the crime.

The witness was aware of the hay rope, which hung from a beam to the threshing floor almost to the ground. Viewed from the courtyard, the rope was in the immediate vicinity of the barn door on the left.

Joseph Mayer
Interviewed on 01/10/1952 and 06/05/1952

The married postman, Joseph Mayer, who resided in Waidhofen was first questioned by detectives in January 1952. Mayer had been working in the postal service in Waidhofen, Schrobenhausen District, since

March 1, 1921, with Gröbern, and Hinterkaifeck falling within his delivery route. The witness stated that he knew the residents at Hinterkaifeck. They were "approachable people". He drove past the property every day and was also in the house once a month since he personally brought Victoria Gabriel her war widow's pension. Mayer delivered the Schrobenhausen weekly newspaper to which the Gabriel/Gruber family subscribed three times a week, on Mondays, Wednesdays and Fridays. It had been agreed with the residents that Mayer would stick the newspaper inside the kitchen window facing the road.

Sometimes one of the residents would be at the oven or well on the northside of the house. On one of these occasions in March 1922, Mayer was approached by both Andreas Gruber and Victoria Gabriel as to whether he had noticed anything odd, as they believed that someone was frequently trespassing. Mayer was asked by one of the two whether anyone in the area subscribed to the "Münchner Zeitung", which he also replied they did not. This was regarding Gruber finding a copy of the paper in the woods near his house.

According to the witness, there was a wintery slush on the ground at this time. When he passed the property, Andreas Gruber and Victoria Gabriel were studying footprints that led from the field path past the north side of the house toward the barn. They reported to the witness that a trail led into the barn, but they could not find anything during the search.

On Friday, March 31, 1922, Mayer handed the newspaper over personally to Andreas Gruber, who had been at the back of the house drawing water. That day he saw Andreas Gruber for the last time. The next delivery of the weekly paper was then on Monday, April 3, 1922. On that day he did not see any of the residents and thus put the newspaper on the kitchen window at around 8:30 a.m.

Mayer insisted that the story of the Friday newspaper being on the kitchen window was not true, since he personally handed it over to Andreas Gruber. He also noticed that on Monday the stroller was not in the kitchen as usual. The kitchen door was half open. The cattle were restless and "grunted", but not loudly mooing. As always, the farm dog did not growl when he put the newspaper by the kitchen window.

Mayer stated he went in and out near the back door. The door had no handle on the outside and could only be opened from the inside. From the back door one first entered an anteroom, from there to the left a door led into the barn and to the right a door led into the kitchen. There was a rotten wooden fence on the north side and on the southside a wire mesh fence.

During a second interrogation in June 1952 before the local court in Schrobenhausen, Mayer added more information after being asked whether he knew other people from the surrounding area who had been in contact with the Hinterkaifeck residents. From January 10th until 1921, a maid named Kreszenz Rieger worked there, who, according to his memory, gave birth to a daughter on a Holy Saturday. In his opinion, Rieger would most likely to be able to provide information about people who were connected to the murder victims. Mayer, testified under oath, once again at his second interrogation that he personally gave the " Schrobenhausener Wochenblatt" to Andreas

Gruber on March 31, 1922. Claims to the contrary, that on April 3, 1922, he found the last newspaper delivered on March 31, 1922 still placed in the window are false.

Johann Schlittenbauer Interviewed
on 01/10/1952

The testimony of Johann Schlittenbauer (born 03/27/1906 Gröbern, died 02/09/1977), the eldest son of, Lorenz Schlittenbauer, was recorded in January 1952. The witness claimed that he could still remember the Hinterkaifeck murders very well. On Tuesday, April 4th, 1922, between 2:00 p.m. and 3:00 p.m., a mechanic came to his parents' property at No. 20 Gröbern and reported to his sisters, Maria and Victoria Schlittenbauer, that he had been to Hinterkaifeck and repaired the engine. The mechanic had asked the two women to inform the family at Hinterkaifeck, since he couldn't find anyone there. The mechanic also said that he had broken into the engine shed in order to be able to fix the engine. Johann Schlittenbauer stated that they talked about the information provided by the mechanic at home during Vespers, around 3:00 to 4:00 p.m.

Lorenz Schlittenbauer then sent the witness, Johann Schlittenbauer, and his younger stepbrother, Joseph Schlittenbauer (born March 31, 1913 Diepoltshofen, died on April 5, 1944, in Russia) to Hinterkaifeck with a message that the engine had been repaired. The witness and his stepbrother, Joseph, arrived at Hinterkaifeck between 3:00 p.m. and 3:30 p.m. All the doors of the farm buildings were locked.

The two of them peered through the windows, but saw no one. According to Johann Schlittenbauer, the newspaper was also in the window. They then went around the house into the courtyard. The dog barked from in the barn when the barn door was shaken. The cattle did not react. The barn door was not locked, but it was closed.

According to Johann Schlittenbauer's testimony, Lorenz Schlittenbauer decided to visit the farm as well. Johann accompanied his father and the neighbors, Pöll and Sigl, to Hinterkaifeck (Jakob Sigl confirmed his testimony). After the bodies were discovered in the barn, the witness was told by his father to inform the mayor in Wangen that the people in Hinterkaifeck had been killed. Joseph Kreitmeier, from Gröbern, who had meanwhile come to Hinterkaifeck by bike, took Johann with him.

On the way people were told that all residents of Hinterkaifeck had been slain, in Wangen the mayor did not believe the news at first, but then alerted police after repeated reports about murder. Then Johann went back to the scene. Numerous onlookers had already gathered there. According to the witness, Lorenz Schlittenbauer, did not want to let people into the house. When the police arrived at Hinterkaifeck, they had cordoned off the scene, but nevertheless many people had already entered the house. Johann did not enter the premises again. He claimed to have not seen the bodies of Joseph Gruber and Maria Baumgartner.

Anton Gump
Interviewed on 05/06/1952

On May 6, 1952, the retired Anton Gump (Born June 11, 1887 Karlskron), married and living in Ingolstadt, was arrested. The former grinder was suspected right off, together with his brother, Adolf Gump (Born 12/04/1889 Karlskron, Died 02/29/1944 Würzburg) on March 31/ April 1, 1922. to have murdered the Hinterkaifeck residents. Gump's home was searched as documented in applications for a arrest warrant dated May 2 and 7, 1952. The arrest was based on the death bed confession of the alleged perpetrator's sister, Kreszentia Mayer, born Gump (Born May 12, 1886, October 20, 1941 Augsburg). She told the story to two clergymen accusing her brothers of the crime.

As Kreszentia Mayer requested, a clergyman wrote down the information on a piece of paper. The information provided by the sister appeared credible to the Augsburg public prosecutor's office and was given under circumstances that would rule out the sister's "false accusations" against her brothers.

The Augsburg Regional Court prosecutor, Dr. Andreas Popp, argued that even without the information provided by the sister, Adolf and Anton Gump's assumption of guilt was "biologically justified. Their father, Anton Gump (senior), had been convicted in 1907 by the Neuburg District Court for drinking. He and his son, Adolf Gump, then travelled around the country in 1908 and 1909 making it impossible for the Neuburg Guardianship Court to determine their whereabouts.

According to police, Anton Gump was employed at the Deutschen Werken in Ingolstadt (around 24 km from Gröbern) at the time in question at the end of March/beginning of April 1922. At that time, his brother worked as a basket maker or basket peddler. The application an arrest warrant dated May 7, 1952 showed that the witness, Magdalena Schindler, Adolf Gump's companion at the time, stated that she and Gump had also come to the area around Schrobenhausen on their travels. According to the witness, Adolf Gump was said to have been alone in the area around Hinterkaifeck in the period after the crime. As stated in the application of May 7, 1952, Anton Gump said when he was arrested that he had never been to the Hinterkaifeck area. To investigators, the fact that he allegedly did not know the town of Waidhofen made him suspicious, although he was employed as a servant for several years in Niederambach, a little more than an hour's walk away.

The investigation against Anton Gump was initiated by a letter to the editor from 19-year-old typesetter, Rudolf Storz, from Munich to the "Schwäbische Landeszeitung". The letter was printed there on November 16, 1951 under the heading "I know the murderers". The writer, who reacted to a report on the unsolved murders at Hinterkaifeck, claimed to know a priest who knew the identity of the Hinterkaifeck killers. The priest refused to speak about it although the secret was communicated outside of confession,

On January 11, 1952, Storz reported to the judge at the Munich District Court that in October 1948, that he and other young people attended a group meeting in the Catholic Youth Home in Weissenhom in the Swabian region of Ulm. The secret of confession came into question. The group leader, Chaplain Anton Hauber, gave an example from his own experience and said that he knew the murderers at Hinterkaifeck by name. Anton Hauber was town chaplain in Augsburg during the war and one day he had a conversation with a woman. After the confession, the terminally ill woman asked him to pick up paper and pencil. Then she dictated two names to him and explained that they were her brothers and that they committed the Hinterkaifeck crimes. She asked the priest to pass the note onto police, which Hauber never did. The reason he gave Storz was that there was a risk that no one would believe that he actually obtained the knowledge outside of confession. He did not want to shake confidence of Catholics in the confessional.

The woman feared for her life because she revealed the secret. Hauber did tell officials the approximate age of the deceased. Since the year of death could be narrowed down to 1940 to 1942 and it was known that the deceased lived in a shack on Derchinger Strasse (Augsburg-Lechhausen) and must have had at least two brothers, the officials managed to use the death certificates stored at the registry office to determine the identity of the woman. On October 20, 1941, a certain Kreszentia Mayer died of cancer in the municipal hospital. The woman's maiden name was "Gump".

The officials discovered that Chief Inspector Reingrubers had already searched for a Gump on April 9, 1922 on suspicion of being involved in a multiple murder in Upper Silesia of nine people. Further investigations by police revealed that August Ritzl, then the parish priest of St. Pankratius in Augsburg-Lechhausen, in whose parish Anton Hauber was a chaplain, knew the Hinterkaifeck family. The ailing Ritzl, was questioned on March 31, 1952 in the Augsburg general hospital. It turned out that in 1940/41 he was called to see a sick person at Derchinger Strasse 120N to hear her confession. Outside of confession, the patient told him that she knew the murderers from Hinterkaifeck and that they were brothers. During his interrogation, Ritzl admitted that he no longer remembered the names of the sick woman or her brothers. But after the name "Gump" was suggested to him during the interrogation, along with other names, he was able to remember it again.

Ritzl said that the woman presented as mentally normal and he had believed her, as in his opinion she wanted to ease her conscience. Public Prosecutor Dr. Popp wanted to be sure and urged Hauber to confirm the names. Positive feedback was received in mid- April in response to a written query sent to Hauber on April 2nd, 1952, to determine whether he had found the note with the names. Hauber submitted a slip of paper on which the names "Adolf and Anton Gump" were noted. A detective was then sent to Weissendorn, where the witness no longer remembered whether the patient said they were her brothers.

During his second interrogation on May 10, 1952, while in custody, Anton Gump stated that he visited his brother Adolf Gump in 1922, who at the time was doing his basket-making business in the area around Schrobenhausen. At the time, his brother was accompanied by a woman whose name he could no longer remember. Anton Gump stated he met this woman twice. He saw the woman for the first time when his brother visited him at home in Ingolstadt. That was around Easter time, which fell on April 16 in 1922.

A few weeks later he visited them on a farm in the area around Schrobenhausen, where Adolf Gump worked as a basket maker. The interviewee could no longer remember the name of the place, but he could describe the route that he took with his bicycle from Ingolstadt. The route led through the village of Brunnen, some 5 km from Gröbern, but he could not recall whether he had turned left there in a south-easterly direction or toward Edelshausen some 4 km away.

Gump could not say exactly how long it took him to get there. However, due to the distance he had to go from his original plan to return to Ingolstadt on the same day, he had to spend the night on the farm along with his brother and his girlfriend in the barn.

During the visit, he learned from his brother that the Hinterkaifeck farm, where the murder took place, was not far away. He had been aware of the murder case as all the newspapers at the time published articles. Anton Gump recalled receiving apples and a ready-to-roast goose from his brother. The next day he rode back to Ingolstadt the same way he came. Gump said he had never been in the area before visiting his brother, Adolf. He was not familiar with the place he visited his brother from his previous employment in Kaltenherberg or Hohenried. Anton Gump described the woman as follows: "Medium height of about five foot, three inches , full, round face, black hair, I estimate the age of this woman to be around 30 years."

The assumption that there was a connection between the Gump brothers and the Hinterkaifeck family was based solely on information provided by Kreszentia Mayer. Beyond the information provided by the two clergymen that the witness made a normal impression and probably wanted to ease her conscience with the information, the credibility of the witness or the origin of the incriminating information were not investigated in more detail. One can assume that Kreszentia Mayer was not an eyewitness to the murder, but rather, heard hearsay and relied on information that third parties told her about events on Hinterkaifeck.

The information given by Kreszentia Mayer regarding the alleged guilt of her brothers was probably not accurate as there was some tension in the family regarding incestuous relationships and it is not certain about the source of the confession to the two priests. It was not unusual for people at the time to point fingers at those they had disputes with in the family or with significant others. Police would track down numerous false accusations, which further wasted valuable time.

On May 29, 1952, Anton Gump was released from pre-trial detention after more than three weeks as a suspect in the Hinterkaifeck murders. Simply being the area was not enough to charge him as he often did agricultural work and had reason to be around Gröbern. On February 1st, 1954 the investigation against Anton Gump was finally dropped.

Heinrich Ney
Interviewed on 01/19/1953

The bailiff at the Kaufbeuren District Court Heinrich Ney (Born November 21, 1895 Neuburg) was called to a judicial hearing on January 19, 1953 and summoned by police on March 20, 1953. Ney stated that from January 1st, 1921 he worked as an assistant to the public prosecutor's office in Neuburg.

In this capacity he, together with Prosecutor Renner, district court coroner, Dr. Aumüller, and a rental car owner, visited the Hinterkaifeck crime scene after being informed by Schrobenhausen police. When they arrived on April 5, 1922, detectives from Munich were already on site. The bodies of the victims were still lying as they were after the crime was committed. The witness could remember that newspapers and letters were stuck outside the kitchen window. In addition, the front door was locked.

As Ney stated, the corpses would be dissected one day later on April 6, 1922 at the Hinterkaifeck farm. The corpses were autopsied on a table in the farm courtyard with the heads of the six victims removed during dissection. The heads were then taken to the Pathological Institute of the University of Munich for further dissection. On behalf of the public prosecutor's office, Ney took the prepared heads to a clairvoyant in Nuremberg, who reported to police after receiving a reward of 100,000 marks that he could name the perpetrators by using the heads. However, the result of the "test" was negative.

During the autopsy of Cecilia Gabriel coroner Dr. Aumüller, explained that the child could have been

128

saved if the crime had been discovered in good time. The girl suffered a throat injury near the carotid artery, which only led to death after 2 to 3 hours. Ney stated that the dissected corpses were returned to the open threshing room floor.

When the body of Cecilia Gabriel was brought back, Ney and the two porters noticed that suddenly a thumb-thick hay rope was hanging from the attic above the threshing room that had not been there before. The porters were so frightened that they almost dropped the stretcher, questioning loudly about where that rope suddenly came from. It was immediately assumed that someone had slid down from the hay loft.

At the top of the dusty crossbeam, two handprints were recognizable from the person who must have lowered himself on the rope. The rope was taunt. The knot that connected the hay rope to the crossbeam was also very tight, from which it was concluded that a considerable load must have been hanging on the rope. Ney claimed to have reported the observation immediately to the judicial commission, which then came to the barn. Despite the use of a tracking dog, nothing could be determined. As Ney added in his interrogation on March 20, 1953, there was fresh snow that day. In a later interrogation, Ney added that the judicial commission had discovered two hollows in the hay, which would have suggested that it must have been a bed for two people. Allegedly human excrement was found near the indentions.

Chapter Eight

Official Reconstruction of the Crime

According to the official investigation results of the police and public prosecutor's office, the following chronology of events can be assumed for March 31, 1922; According to Munich detectives, the crime was committed by several perpetrators, who were assumed to be career criminals.

From the footprints that were found, which led from the forest towards Hinterkaifeck, but not back again, it was concluded that the perpetrators went to the property before March 31, 1922. Only after the crime, or after the snow had melted at the end of the month, did they leave the farm.

The perpetrators arrived on the night of March 30 or March 31, 1922 via the unlocked gate, which was only locked with a wooden wedge from the outside, into the northern part of the machine house and entered the barn.

The perpetrators initially hid in the attic above the barn. The perpetrators reach the attic via a ladder attached to the western barn wall. They waited in the attic for a suitable opportunity for the robbery. One could watch the farm area through the roof tiles pushed aside. Impressions can be seen in the hay, as if one or more people stayed there for some time.

As the residents never left the house or the property for any length of time during the day, the perpetrators left their hiding place in the hayloft after 8:00 p.m. on the evening of March 31, 1922. They untied a young cow in the adjacent barn to lure the residents into the barn.

Victoria Gabriel, Cecilia Gruber, Andreas Gruber and little Cilli Gabriel entered the feed room and the adjacent barn one after the other. Immediately behind the connecting door to the barn, the residents are killed by targeted blows on the head with a blunt weapon. From the barn, the perpetrators entered the living quarters through the feed room.

In the residential wing, Maria Baumgartner was killed in her room first. Then the perpetrators entered Victoria Gabriel's bedroom, where the two-year-old Joseph Gruber was butchered in his stroller.

The victim's clothing and the situation in which they were found suggest a time before going to bed, sometime between 8:00 p.m. and 11 p.m.

After a forensic investigation, the mattock, which was found during demolition work on March 29, 1923, was the main weapon. The different patterns of injuries on the victim's heads, from detective's view, indicate the use of several tools. According to later evaluations by police, a band iron and a pocket knife could also be weapons, which were also found when Hinterkaifeck was torn down along with the mattock seized on 04/04/1922 over the feed room.

According to investigators, the perpetrators stole paper money from Victoria Gabriel's bedroom worth an estimated 100,000 marks (corresponding to an equivalent amount of around EUR 34,000). Greed was therefore a possible motive for the crime. After the crime, the killers stayed on the property for some time, possibly until the evening of April 1st, 1922. Farmers on surrounding farms, who were busy with the spring cultivation, did not notice any disturbance of the cattle on Hinterkaifeck. The investigators assumed that the perpetrators looking after the cattle in order to prevent early detection of the crime.

The murder weapon, a mattock, was hidden under the floorboards in the loft above the living area near the stairs. During their stay, the perpetrators removed half a piece of smoked meat from the smokehouse in the attic for consumption on site.

The killers left the property the same way they entered, namely through the feed room, the adjacent barn and from there through the machine house.

According to the investigators, the four corpses lying in the barn were covered with hay and a door so that the murderers could walk unhindered over the corpses on their way back through the barn.

Chapter Nine

The Search for Motives

Prosecutor Ferdinand Renner studied old criminal cases searching for motives to the butchery. In 1922 Andreas Gruber and the widowed Victoria Gabriel sat in jail charged with incest. Victoria, who had turned a few men's heads in her life, had sexual relations with her own father for many years from her sixteenth birthday onwards. In 1913 she was deeded the farm by her parents. At that time Victoria was twenty-six. The farm had been the dowry for her widowed mother's second marriage to Andreas Gruber who was nine-years younger than Cecilia.

A few weeks after Victoria had become an heir, she married the one year younger, Karl Gabriel, from Laag a few miles south of Hinterkaifeck. The farm may have been signed over to her for a dowry. But happiness was short-lived and the relationship cooled rapidly. On August 14, 1914, when Karl

Gabriel was suddenly summoned to the Kösching recruiting station near Ingolstadt, divorce had already been discussed.

In the first year of the war the expectant father died on the Western Front. This was on December 12, 1914, in a battle at Neuville in France. His body was never recovered and buried properly as it lay in a bombed-out trench along with other troops. Only a few weeks later Victoria gave birth to her first child. She was christened Cecilia after her grandmother.

Renner studied the verdict of May 28, 1915, in which Andreas Gruber had been sentenced to one year imprisonment for incest and his daughter, Victoria Gabriel, to one month. Prior to age sixteen she had not been charged as she was a minor. Underneath it stated: "Both have served their sentences." But the father and daughter were not considered redeemed by everyone. The name of the Gröbern town official, Lorenz Schlittenbauer, appeared several times in the documents. In July 1918, after his first wife had died from breast cancer, he wanted to marry Victoria Gabriel. The widow did not object, but her father would not allow it.

On September 7, 1919 she gave birth to an illegitimate son, Joseph. She listed Lorenz Schlittenbauer as the father. He had seduced her in the hay only two weeks after the death of his first wife, also named Victoria. But people whispered that the child belonged to no other than grandpa Gruber. Out of anger over the marriage denial, Schlittenbauer accused Victoria of incest three days after childbirth and her father along with her. The 63-year-old Gruber was detained immediately because he had been previously convicted of incest. Less than three weeks later, Schlittenbauer, after pleading by Victoria, changed his mind. At a hearing on September 30 before the guardianship court in Schrobenhausen, he cleared Andreas Gruber and stated he was father of little Joseph. But as soon as

Andreas Gruber was released, Schlittenbauer denied paternity again. The story was a precursor to Peyton Place.

George Reingrubers burned the midnight oil writing his report at the Munich police headquarters. In Reingrubers opinion, there had been a large amount of paper money kept at Hinterkaifeck immediately before the crime.

Since the Gabriel/Gruber family, as the owners of a larger farm at that time, were considered wealthy from investigators' point of view, greed was an obvious motive for the crime. In addition to fixed-income securities with a nominal value of 15,100 marks, gold and silver coins, as well as gold and silver jewelry, were not taken by the killers. With inflation being high, it was strange that the intruder did not take the secure silver and gold in favor of paper currency. The appearance of being in a hurry prompted police to assume it was a robbery gone bad. The thieves took the easiest property to carry.

The house did not have the overall impression of being ransacked, except for the closet in Victoria's room. In Victoria's bedroom the perpetrators apparently searched for something particular. Reingrubers had carefully pulled back the upper bed covers during the search. He remarked to Criminal Secretary Andreas Biegleder, "Look at what's all there." Randomly thrown on the white sheet, was an empty wallet, a notebook, several contract notes, a few sheets of paper inscribed in ink, and a ladies' wristwatch. The authorities concluded that the perpetrators may had been interrupted during the crime, which was why mainly paper money was stolen due to time constraints.

As one of the first suspects, on April 7, 1921, a baker named Joseph Bärtl from Geisenfeid near Ingolstadt was suspected because he had escaped from the Günzburg sanatorium. Due to the atrocity of the crime, the public prosecutor's office determined that only a mentally ill person could be the perpetrator. Could they really have been killed for a few thousand or even tens of thousands of marks? And why the maid, why the two children? Was he the child of Schlittenbauer or Andreas Gruber? The death of the boy disturbed him. On page five of his seven-page report, Reingrubers wrote:

"Why the murderer also killed the two-year-old boy cannot be explained (Some sources say eighteen months). The child could have been no threat. It could be that the murderer was a person known to the child by name, or the child had made a noise. Possibly the child had been killed due to family interests. In brackets, he added the word" inheritance".

Another idea that kept hounding George Reingrubers was not as far-fetched as it first seemed. Wonder if the husband of Victoria Gabriel was not killed in the war? If he recently came back with prisoner transports from France and saw that his wife had again become a mother that could be a motive. Sergeant Ludwig Meixl of the Schrobenhausen auxiliary police had instigated the investigation. In a letter he had urgently asked the Munich Police to request the appropriate authorities in Bavaria to determine whether Karl Gabriel was in a transport of prisoners just before the murders. Karl Gabriel was reported to have been scene in Gröbern in 1918. It was not unusual for soldiers to be reported killed in action or missing and then show up at home months later during World War I and previous wars. Communication and transportation were poor.

Chief Inspector Ramer immediately contacted the Central Office for evidence of War Casualties and War Graves on the Oberwiesenfeld in Munich. The answer from there was clear. Karl Gabriel was buried in the trench with members of his former company near Neuville in northern France. So quickly, a very hot lead turned cold for Reingrubers. The document, which lay on his desk, was signed by the then commander of the 13th Bavarian Infantry Regiment, in which Karl Gabriel had belonged in the 6th Company. Ramer and Reingrubers did not have any evidence to dispute this fact. Twenty-one years later the theory would again surface.

A story told by a former soldier vacationing in Russia would cause the Augsburg police to investigate the murders again in 1943. The witness with the story began;

"I'll start now. Karl Gabriel is still living in Russia today. He is even said to be enlisted by the Russians as a commissar (political officer) in the current war". This was revealed by a front-line soldier on furlough in a pub in Schrobenhausen. The soldier had been in Russian captivity with several comrades a few months ago. The commissar who heard them, had immediately recognized the dialect and knew the prisoners came from Bavaria when they called out their hometowns. When at Ebenhausen near Ingolstadt, the commissar asked if they had heard of Hinterkaifeck. Then he steered the conversation to the murders.

The commissar stated that he was the murderer and there was no need to keep look for the offender. He had killed his family because his wife gave birth to a baby during his absence with her biological father. After this confession, the officer released the prisoners and sent them back to the German troops. Revenge and jealousy could be a motive that would explain a great deal. The witness signed the document. Then police stations were alerted locally to determine who the frontline traveler was who had met Karl Gabriel in Russia.

Somehow the press got wind of it and The " Aichacher Zeitung" prepared a sprawling article under the headline, "Light Shed on Murder after 21 Years"' Readers learned what some had always suspected: that some other soldier must have been killed in France in 1914.

The article, began "21 years ago, a murder on the remote Hinterkaifeck farm, in which a whole family fell victim, caused a great stir. The murderer escaped at that time and could not be located. This killer has now surprisingly been exposed. Three soldiers from the Schrobenhausen area who came home from the eastern front reported this adventurous story: During a melee they were taken with others into Soviet captivity. The commanding Soviet commissar now asked all prisoners whether people from Schrobenhausen were among them. When our three informants came forward, he confessed to them that he was the wanted murderer of Hinterkaifeck and, to prevent an innocent from having to pay for his act, he released the three Schrobenhausen men. The murderer, who was none other than the husband of the murdered Victoria, had been taken as a Russian prisoner of war during the First World War.

In 1922 he had managed to escape by fleeing to his homeland. In Munich, he stayed overnight during his escape, and there he happened to find out that his wife had lived on the isolated farm with another man and had borne his children. He was so angry that he went home immediately and killed his wife in the middle of the night along with a stranger, children and a maid for a total of seven persons, with a pickaxe". The fact that he named seven victims should have been a red flag.

"After the deed he ransacked the entire house for money and valuables to give the impression of a robbery. In order not to be betrayed when fleeing by animal cries in the barn, he had given the animals food for two days. Before the crime, he had been hiding in the hayloft for five days to spy on the whole situation. After the crime he fled back to Russia, where, as a result of his cruel behavior, he was brought to the People's Commissar. This was the sort of person Stalin was recruiting".

The editor still had reservations about the story and wondered about the sudden leniency of the commissar: "With the population of Schrobenhausen, however, the investigation of these murders will cause no less a sensation and surprise as the bloody act 21 years ago," he continued. "We print this story, which was told in our district area and whose accuracy we cannot guarantee, with all reservations. It is strange that the cruel commissar suddenly discovered his conscience and his soft heart, which could only be explained by the fact that he must have been German. It would also be conceivable that in this way he wanted to be famous in his homeland."

In the end the article did not go to print due to the number of errors such as stating the number of victims as seven and not six. This mistake has led some speculation that there was a suitor waiting for Victoria outside when the murders occurred, thus a missing body.

On May 17, 1943, the publisher of the "Aichacher Zeitung" informed Schrobenhausen police: "Under consultation and instruction of the Deputy General Command VII at Munich, we have shelved the article until final verification of the facts has taken place." Searches for the Russian commissar were futile as well as locating the men who allegedly talked to him. The local police reported on June 3, 1943 to Augsburg court: "Neither the source nor service of such a narrative by those soldiers is known."

It did not stop people from wondering about the story of Karl Gabriel's fate. There will always be doubters who continue to ponder whether the Russian soldier was indeed Gabriel and did he extract revenge. The theory came up again a few years later.

On November 3, 1951, Matthäus Eser from Ingolstadt was interviewed by the editor-in-chief, Norbert Mayer in the editorial offices of the "Danube Courier Am Stein" number 12.

"Well, the things about Hinterkaifeck, as you write it, are not always true," he began. Eser told the retired journalist what he experienced after his capture on May 24, 1945 on a dusty country road in Bohemia. Using plastic models, Eser captivated his audience. Soon he was drawn into the fascinating events that were said to have taken place about 30 kilometers north of Neuhaus.

A scattered German unit was on the run from the advancing Russians. In tattered uniforms, emaciatcd and devoid of any illusions, a troop of soldiers and a nurse were headed North towards the Americans and away from the Russians. A younger corporal cracked a joke to lighten the mood. "When we get home, we all become honorary members of the "Ramblers Association!" Nobody found it funny and one soldier growled "idiot" at him.

Then they heard engine noises. The soldiers, including Matthew Eser of the 71st Infantry Division, threw themselves into ditches on both sides of the road. In vain however. as the approaching Russians had spotted them miles back. Then everything happened very fast. The Germans were rounded up and searched for weapons. Finally, they had to stand with their hands behind their necks in rows of three. In the open field, the Russians set up a makeshift camp and posted sentries. It was hot and time dragged on. Suddenly the guards shouted something. Then a senior officer appeared, a commissar with his uniform jacket adorned with medals. The Russian passed by them with a scowl.

Eser asked his comrade, Fritz Herrmann: "You think I'm going back to Russia now?"

A nurse named Erika from Regensburg, who stood next to them, asked: "What will they do with us now?"

It seemed like the Russian commissar understood her German, but he ignored her and went on. A little while later, Eser asked one of the guards for something to eat. When he did not understand, he used sign language. But the Russian shook his head and pointed to where the commissar stood. Eser hesitated for several minutes, but then obeyed. He stood at attention before the commissar, who surveyed him solemnly from top to bottom.

Even before Eser could reply, the commissar asked in authentic Bavarian: 'Where are you from?"

Eser was speechless and it took a few seconds before he could answer: "From Schrobenhausen."

"Yes, yes, Schrobenhausen," replied the Russian, "I know that place too".

Without worrying about the prisoner any further, the commissar turned around and walked away. When Matthäus Eser returned to the other prisoners, they were eating bread. A little later, the soldiers began marching again. As they plodded apathetically toward Russian captivity, Eser wondered about the Bavarian-speaking Russian. He could not figure it out. There was a short break in the late hot afternoon. Exhausted, the men fell over where they stood.

Everyone was very thirsty from choking down dirt. Eser decided to ask the commissar for water who leaned against the open door of his command vehicle with his eyes half closed. Again, Eser respectfully approached the officer and stood at attention. When the Russian peered at him, he asked for a drink of water. The commissar reached into the car and handed him a canteen. Eser gulped water while the Russian watched him closely and then asked abruptly, "Are you familiar with Waidhofen?"

Eser nearly gagged at odd question. He knew Waidhofen well as he spent part of his youth there.

The commissar asked again: "Then you know Gröbern?" And without waiting for the answer, he added, "And ... a... Hinterkaifeck?"

Eser was stunned. Only after some time he nodded. As a boy, he has often been to the farm. Old Gruber, in particular, let him in when he once asked for potatoes. He now told the commissar everything he knew about the remote agricultural area. The farm was no longer there, and people still suspected each other of being a murderer. Even as Eser spoke, the commissioner turned and left, which seemed weird. Why ask if you do not want an answer?

After a few minutes he returned and put a paper form in his hand. It was a pass. The commissar told him. "And if someone asks you, say the murderer of Hinterkaifeck has released you."

Even before the commissar left, Eser requested that his comrades, Fritz Hermann from Magdeburg and the Regensburg nurse, be included on the pass. Without waiting for a thank you, the commissar climbed into his vehicle. Eser was baffled. He stood there with his two companions on the road and watched as the other prisoners gathered on command and marched east toward a Russian prison camp. With the pass from the commissar, the three went freely through all Russian road blocks. After two days at Linz, Austria they reached American occupied territory.

On June 3, 1945, Eser was back home in Ingolstadt. The returning soldier signed a declaration that his statements corresponded to the whole truth. He described how as a boy he had run with dozens of other curious people to the murder farm. The victims had been right where they had been killed.

He was horrified and ran out of Victoria's room after seeing the stroller with the shattered roof and the corpse of little Joseph. In the next room there was a man who rummaged through a bundle of letters and did not notice him at first. Presumably there were letters that Victoria had received from her husband from the field or even later. The man read it visibly agitated. Eser stood so close to him that he overheard a few lines. Two sentences stuck in his head.

"Well, if that's true, after what I've learned" and "society is rotten". When the man saw that Eser was reading along, he pushed the boy away violently, tore up the letter and put in it in the trash.

"Sensational Turn" was the headline of the " Danube Courier". The caption read: "Will the Puzzle be Solved after 30 Years?" The account of Eser's short story ended with the words: "We did not expect this turn of events, which seems likely to solve the mystery of the murderer. However, that may be, the man who accuses himself of murdering those six people lives far away from Germany. He has, if he is really the murderer, no earthly jurisdiction to fear. But he has not escaped his conscious and guilt in his own heart".

Of course, such news was of interest to everyone, including other reporters in Augsburg. Court reporter, Alfons A. Schertl from the "Swabian National" newspaper went to Ingolstadt and interviewed Matthäus Eser. He again retold the surprising encounter with the Russian commissar again.

Schertl inquired about Eser's opinion of who the 55 to 60-year-old Russian could have been. The reporter seeded the answer with the question, "You also knew Karl Gabriel, who married Victoria?"

Eser answered carefully: "Yes, I can remember him. I have often thought about it. If I consider the age and if I imagine the face under the uniform cap, I would say that it could have been him."

Schertl quizzed Eser for some time, trying to test him with various questions, but he continued to answer, "I don't know".

Eser could have fed the reporter whatever stories he felt like that Schertl could not verify at the time, but he did not embellish. This convinced the journalist that Eser was legit and not lying. The information from Eser was very specific and detailed and had the tone of someone who was there. Schertl was also in the Second World War. While both men knew that Karl Gabriel officially died in 1914, they also knew that many an officially dead person reappeared.

So, what can police do with such stories being possibly true? Comrades of Karl Gabriel state they saw him standing near the trench that was hit by a mortar, a state-of-the-art weapon in World War I. It was not unusual for dozens of soldiers to be buried in the trenches meant to shield them. The Bayonet Trench at Verdun is a prime example. The commander of Gabriel's regiment signed a statement that the man fell in France, yet why would a Russian officer claim credit for a brutal crime that could in no way benefit him?

If he was Gabriel, then Karl was the type of killer that wanted people to know what he did, and thus released local German soldiers back to their homes near Hinterkaifeck to spread the word. Was he a serial killer or what is known as a "family annihilator", who wipes out his entire family then starts over again somewhere else?" Police never discovered the name of this mysterious Russian commissar, so tracking him would be nearly impossible.

If Eser's story is true then it is also disturbing that even children strolled through a bloody crime scene with no adult restraining them. Are we to assume then that the man with the letter was Karl Gabriel still hanging around the crime scene? Talk about hiding in plain sight. What is interesting is that some European troops were issued clubs embedded with spikes that would cause similar injuries as the Hinterkaifeck victims.

****

Robbery was the first motive police assumed when arriving at the crime scene, which was not unreasonable with the mess left in Victoria's room. This assumption, however, led investigators in the wrong direction wasting valuable time. The number of items left behind exclude robbery as the primary motive.

The Schrobenhausen notary, Albert Stinglwagner, of the Honorary Justice Council drew up an inventory of valuables found at the crime scene;

> ➢ 1880 goldmarks, mostly in twenty Reichsmark pieces
> ➢ 327 silver marks, some aluminum and nickel coins as well as ten pfennig pieces (war money) in the value of exactly 5.10 marks
> ➢ 16 bank notes, among other things from the commercial bank, the Bavarian land credit, the Frankfurt am Main railway and the Ungarian railway, most of which are valued at a thousand marks
> ➢ Passbooks of Andreas Gruber and the child, Cecilia, from the Waidhofen Loan-Cash Association.
> ➢ But also some jewelry had been found at the crime scene.
> ➢ Two silver men's watches
> ➢ two ladies' watches,
> ➢ two gold rings with opal stones,
> ➢ two wedding rings,
> ➢ a coral brooch,
> ➢ a long silver necklace
> ➢ strings of pearls

- gold earrings
- The evidence was kept at Schobenhausen. Nothing appeared to be missing from the house. A fur stole was still there and two candlesticks, a small clock and coffee grinder.

If robbery was the main goal of the killer, a brute who felt comfortable enough to hang around for days caring for livestock and smoked meat with bloody bodies around him, then why would such a person rush around and leave most of the loot behind?

Chapter Ten

The Inheritance Question and the Fate of the Hinterkaifeck Property

On June 7, 1922, the Schrobenhausen District Court awarded the Gruber family all assets of the murder victims. This would seem to have settled the matter, but money issues can cause conflicts and hard feelings in families.

The step-sister of Victoria Gabriel, Cecilia Starringer, who was married and lived in the area received half the property. Bernhard Gruber, one of Andreas's brothers who had lived on the farm property until recently, was satisfied with his one tenth. The rest of the assets were distributed among eleven heirs which included Andreas' brothers Leonhard and Joseph and their sister. The gold and silver coins found at the crime scene were confiscated by the tax office. A letter from the treasury indicated that the money owed was due to tax evasion, the emergency levy and capital gains tax.

Just when matters appeared to be settled Karl Gabriel's father hired a lawyer. The murdered widow was his daughter-in-law, and seven-year-old Cecilia was her only matrimonial child making her his granddaughter.

Since her last name was Gabriel, Cecilia would have inherited the Hinterkaifeck property. The attorney argued that the girl had died after her mother. This would have made Karl Gabriel Senior his grandchild's heir. The Neuburg Regional Court disagreed and found that Victoria Gabriel and little Cecilia "had perished in common danger as defined by § 20 BGB". The girl was ruled out of the succession. Several unsuccessful appeals followed and a petition for injunction was rejected by the judges as well. Karl Gabriel Senior wanted to prevent the eleven Gruber heirs from freely disposing of "movable and immovable property," as his lawyer stated it. Gabriel continued to fight the issue, but by July 29, the Supreme Court of Appeals of Munich declared the succession to be legally valid.

All inventory, the closets filled with clothes or linens, the sewing machine, four harrows, two plows, 25 chickens, 23 quintals of rye, as well as, 250 pounds of potatoes in the cellar went to the Grubers. After all the hassle, however, the two contending parties sat down together and agreed that the Gabriel family could buy the farm with all the outbuildings for a special price.

George Reingrubers wondered why Karl Gabriel Senior was so insistent on owning the murder house and willing to pay for it. He wanted to demolish it all anyway. Did he not want the farm sold? Or was he just tired of gawkers combing the farm like a sideshow? It would have been helpful to know exactly what Karl had told his family about life at Hinterkaifeck.

Under blizzard conditions, Charles Gabriel senior, his three sons and several neighbors, began demolition in February

1923. They covered the roof and stacked the bricks, rafters and purlins for removal. A team of oxen delivered the old building materials over two kilometers to Laag to the Gabriel farm where a new barn was to be built.

Michael Plöckl Sr. was among the workers from nearby Haidhof. He had given Maria Baumgartner directions to Hinterkaifeck. He was skittish about removing the floorboards from the barn where the bloody victims had laid. The demolition had been going on for several weeks when Joseph Gabriel found an apparently homemade mattock under the planks of the hayloft over the feed room. By then only the exterior walls of the building remained.

Joseph Gabriel shouted to the others and showed them a blood-stained tool that he held up. Plöckl recalled later that he felt a shiver down his spine and it must have been obvious as Joseph stated, "It's all right, that must be the murder weapon. I think the detectives still need it. I'll put it aside and tell the Hohenwart police. Then they can come get it. "

The men studied the poorly crafted tool. "It was definitely made by old Gruber himself," said one of the Gabriel brothers. "Then he was actually killed by his own hand." At the other end of the loft, the perpetrators must have removed a floorboard and pushed the mattock underneath. The men also found a rusted pocket knife along with it.

On February 28, Watch Commander Heinrich Hagel from the Hohenwart police informed the public prosecutor in Neuburg that a bloodstained mattock was still at Hinterkaifeck. After receiving the report at the District Court of Schrobenhausen, second prosecutor, Hensolt, did not think a judicial hearing was necessary, but ordered a sketch of the mattock be made instead. Fortunately, the next day, the first prosecutor, Ferdinand Renner, intervened. He requested the Munich police investigate the possible murder weapon for fingerprints and blood evidence. Three days later, the fingerprinting under Inspector Rubin was completed on March 6th. On March 13, the Munich police department complained to the Hohenwart police that the mattock had still not been submitted as evidence.

Sergeant Hagel informed the Munich police headquarters on March 15: "The mattock in question was delivered by me personally on the order of the District Court of Schrobenhausen on March 2 in the morning." So, chain of evidence was lacking.

In the new forensic laboratories on Ettstrasse the mattock was finally examined for fingerprints. After division Ib found no usable fingerprints, the mattock remained at the Forensic-Medical Institute of the University of Schillerstrasse. There was a delay in processing it as Professor Dr. Hermann Merkel had just started a short vacation. He eventually confirmed the dreaded suspicion that it was the real murder weapon. In addition to human blood sticking to it there was also human, cat or rabbit hair.

A former servant at Hinterkaifeck removed all doubt about the tool's origins. Twenty-year-old George remembered exactly how old Gruber himself carved the handle for the "Reuthaue" in 1918. George had come to Hinterkaifeck at sixteen and remained there only twelve weeks. The actual pick, the iron part, Gruber had attached with two metal strips to the handle. Thus, the sharp-edged piece of metal could not fly off. He drove two screws through the bands in the handle, which was totally "unprofessional", as the former servant remarked. He had noticed this when the old Gruber was working on the tool.

As if the investigation of the Hinterkaifeck murders were not disorganized enough, the Police Chief Josef Ramer on February 8, died suddenly of a stroke during an interrogation at age 61. Since Ramers's death, police officer, Wilhelm Frick, had been temporarily directing the criminal department. Ramer had overseen the Hinterkaifeck murder case and the ongoing investigation in the Sandmayr case, along with many other open cases. Frick would be replaced by a permanent director who would then have to familiarize himself with the cases, taking even more time that the investigators did not have to solve the murders.

The crime scene demolition only further crippled any future investigation or prosecution for the murders. Since only five photographs were taken, studying the crime scene from them is limited. The fact that so many people entered the property not only contaminated the scene, but it is hard to know if people removed any items from the house or outbuildings. More than likely this was the case.

May 23, 1934, on a rural road in Bienville Parish, Louisiana, Bonnie Parker and Clyde Barrow were mowed down by police. When their riddled bodies, still slumped in the stolen car, were pulled through the city streets people reached in and grabbed watches, rings, tore off pieces of clothing, and took anything else available in full view of police and reporters. Hinterkaifeck had the same fascination for people in Germany. People took trains long distances just to examine the gory murder scene, even after nothing was left to see.

It does not seem likely that inheritance was a motive for the gruesome murders. Were they better off than most? Yes, but not enough for murder since most of the heirs had to divide it ten ways. The stepsister primarily benefitted, but since she loaned money to Victoria, Cecilia Starringer and her husband must have been financially comfortable. The money owed probably persuaded the court to award her the larger portion of the estate. In the end, the Gruber and Gabriel families settled the estate among themselves.

The questions regarding money are, why did Victoria close the accounts? Why did she leave 700 gold marks in the church confessional? Why borrow money when they had plenty enough for the new barn and machinery?

Chapter Eleven

Paul Mueller and Other Possible Killers

One scenario might be that Victoria had plans to leave her unpleasant family life. She had emptied out bank accounts six months prior to the murders, so that there was more cash than usual on the farm. Since her child, Cilli, had told classmates that her grandfather hit her mother it was quite probable that this was not an isolated incident. Running screaming into the woods after being beaten would support habitual abuse. Victoria had mentioned to Schlittenbauer that her father constantly badgered her for sex. The fact that the Grubers could not seem to keep maids makes one wonder why, especially since one former maid complained of her room being haunted and someone rattling her door knob. Perhaps Andreas had more than one victim besides his daughter.

The talk about Victoria being promiscuous or "easy" would not be unusual in someone who has been sexually abused for years. Such victims can learn to use their sexuality to obtain what they need as that is what it takes to appease controlling abusers. With the large numbers of servants and farmhands coming through every season she would have had ample opportunity to find someone willing to help her, or take advantage of her, as the case may be. Victoria was said to be attractive with no shortage of suitors, a fact not appreciated by her father.

Her husband Karl had mentioned to people that life on the Gruber place was intolerable as they were mean, dirty and stingy with food. Karl also described children being locked in the cellar, who did not survive to adulthood. He was desperate enough to return to his parents' house and consider divorce early in the marriage. The home life at Hinterkaifeck was disturbing to say the least. Police should have investigated this situation and failed to do so. Residents of Gröbern knew of the other children too and must not have informed authorities. This was a small community and people tended to mind their own business in the past. What exactly happened to the Gruber's other offspring? Why was Victoria the only child that lived to adulthood?

While it is entirely believable that Victoria planned to escape her situation, the fact that she was not dressed for freezing weather would suggest that something interrupted her plans. It has been suggested that she had a boyfriend waiting for her outside. Both she and the children were wearing night clothes as was Andreas. Cecilia Gruber still wore a skirt and apron, so perhaps she was still cleaning up when the killer started his rampage or she had just not changed yet. Someone might well have known Victoria had such plans and knew about the money and valuables in her room. It is also possible that whomever stayed in the attic initially was going to help her and betrayed Victoria instead.

The maid, Maria Baumgartner, was still dressed because she had not unpacked her travel bag and was probably killed right before starting the task. The killer appeared to not have been aware of a stranger being in the house, though it was known in the area that the Grubers were seeking a new maidservant. Witnesses stated that the pot on the stove with the bread soup was untouched indicating that the family never got to sit down and eat. Why would a killer not wait until they were in bed and asleep? It would make more since if the victims had been allowed to eat supper, which tends to make people sleepy and then attack them when they are the most vulnerable after retiring.

The fact that none of the victims had defensive wounds and were struck in the face, suggests they were killed by surprise or laying down. However, there should have been massive blood splatter and pooling if that was the case. The little girl, Cilli, may have awakened during her attack or heard commotion in the house and got up, since she was hit under the chin and not directly in the face. Her cranium was smashed after the initial blow to the neck under her jaw. She also grabbed a handful of her own hair in pain. Was it really her own hair? The autopsy report stated nothing about hair being missing from her scalp.

Another suggestion has been put forth that a man named, Paul Mueller, was the killer. Mueller was a suspect in the United States for multiple murders starting in 1898 to 1912 throughout the country with many similarities to the Hinterkaifeck murders. He was a carpenter and farm hand that preferred to work in isolated areas near railroad tracks. Mueller was also known as a wood cutter.

A short man with dark, greasy hair and small teeth with gaps in between, he did not give people a good feeling. He dressed like a tramp and probably was most of the time hopping trains, but even when given a place to stay for room and board he did nothing to improve his hygiene.

Mueller made a leg brace for his employer's horse when it broke a leg and it did heal well. The horse owner, Francis Newton, was believed to be Mueller's first victim along with his family. It was not common at the time to treat horses with broken bones as they tend to have slow deaths after injuring their legs and are usually put down. Mueller stated that he learned the trick in the army during the war. Which war is not certain as Mueller would not have been old enough for any major war prior to WWI. He may have been in the service, just not in combat.

He was known to be agreeable, but also sullen and cranky. Mueller seemed to have an issue with larger, stronger men, the "little man" complex. He hated his employer, Francis Newton, who was a huge man who ordered Mueller around and treated him poorly, at least from Mueller's standpoint.

He was also considered a suspect in the infamous, Villisca murders in Iowa on June 9, 1912 by the authors of the book, "The Man From the Train". The family of Josiah and Sarah Moore were butchered as they slept, as well their two young guests, Ina and Lena Stillinger. As at Hinterkaifeck, the killer targeted the victims' heads which were "beaten to a pulp". There was a total of nine victims. The house was locked up leading people to assume the killer left through a window. The authors, Bill James and Rachel McCarthy James are certain that Mueller was responsible for fourteen crimes; the Newtons, Lyerlys, Hughneses, Mesowses, Hoods, Schultzes, Casaways, Hills, Burnhams, Waynes, Dawsons, Showmans, Hudsons and the Moores. The last crime Mueller may have committed was the Pfanschmidt family murders in September 1912 and they believe he may have then gone south to New Orleans and caught a freighter bound for Europe. The James' do not exclude Mueller as the killer at Hinterkaifeck.

Police also theorized that he boarded a ship in New York for Europe after 1912. At any rate, though many men matching his description were questioned and arrested, Paul Mueller was never found. It is possible that Mueller could have continued murdering people after returning to Europe. He would have been about sixty at the time of the Hinterkaifeck crime. Used to hard manual labor, Mueller would have been in good physical shape, so still capable of violent crime. Serial killers rarely just stop murdering for no reason. Paul Mueller may not have been his real name either.

Andreas Gruber was a wife beater, forced sex on his daughter, was stingy with food for his family and employees, treated his son-in-law bad and could have provided a trigger for Mueller to butcher the family, if indeed he was in Germany in 1922 and worked for them.

Some interesting facts about Mueller's crimes compared to Hinterkaifeck;

- Murdered with a tool in isolated, thinly populated areas.
- Worked at farms near railroads. The Munich-Ingolstadt railway was near Hinterkaifeck.
- Targeted victims' heads.
- Murdered victims while they slept. (Would make sense at Hinterkaifeck too. Why was there little blood in the house then?)
- Used blunt end of tool most of the time.
- Bodies moved with no obvious purpose.
- Underaged females involved. Some sexually assaulted. No reference to this for Cilli, but she may have struggled prompting the blow from the weapon under her jaw.

- Some things stolen but robbery not the motive. Jewelry left at the crime scene.
- Neighbors noticed livestock had not been fed. They had been fed at Hinterkaifeck, but not enough.
- Murders all committed late at night.
- Murder weapon found on site.
- Houses set on fire or attempted arson. Hinterkaifeck was burned in 1923 by unknown person. It was then demolished shortly after.

****

There were other possible suspects closer to home as well. Detective Chief Inspector Josef Rubner at the Munich police headquarters lab examined the murder weapon and the pickaxe found in the feed room for fingerprints. On February 9, 1925 Rubner wrote a report on the Hinterkaifeck murder case regarding an earlier case no one else had considered.

Rubner stated that they should look at a robber gang which had been exposed in 1903 in Munich. It was nineteen years before the Hinterkaifeck murders, but they were very similar. Josef Schmaderer was the leader, who had pillaged Germany from the Allgäu to the Bavarian Forest. Schmaderer had used his son and daughter as accomplices. His wife was even considered the mastermind behind the whole family gang. At the time, Rubner was still a Chief Inspector in Unit II and recalled that most of the main perpetrators had either avoided punishment by suicide, or had been eliminated by their own cronies. Even the 55-year-old

Josef Schmaderer was said to have hung himself in the police jail.

Police wanted to prove that he was also involved in the quadruple murder and robbery in 1893 in Salmdorf, about eleven kilometers east of Munich, near Riem. Anna Reitsberger, a farmer and widow and her three daughters aged 23, 16 and 14 years were viciously murdered. Rubner saw comparisons between the Salmdorf and Hinterkaifeck cases. As in Hinterkaifeck, the victims had been slain at night in their beds. (In what report did he see this mentioned?) It seemed then that some investigators did think the Hinterkaifeck victims had been butchered in their sleep. The perpetrators burned the farm after the bloody attack, the remains of which were then demolished and never rebuilt.

Rubner saw other frightening parallels to Hinterkaifeck as well. The gang had never brought any weapons, but used what they found as a murder tool. A philosophy of old Schmaderer was supposed to have been, "Just kill, never shoot. Striking makes almost no noise." They raided almost exclusively larger farm estates or stately rectories. Their Modus Operandi was predictable. The perpetrators entered the barn, untied a cow, and then lured their victims to their deaths. Their main concern was primarily money and jewelry. Josef Schmaderer regularly took the train to Munich, melting the spoils at the Royal Bavarian Mint. He owned a business license for the gold and silver trade, so the behavior was not unusual.

For years, the police stumbled around in the dark until a young man was caught in Stuttgart, who later hanged himself in the cell. He thought that the

159

officials had connected him with the quadruple murders. Only after that could it be proved that he had worked with Schmaderer. A mysterious incident at the border in Salzburg was connected. Police had shot a man who violently resisted during the arrest and tried to flee. After a few weeks, it was clear why the initially unknown man tried to escape: He had been a member of the 13-member gang and would have been involved in the quadruple murders.

Schmaderer possessed a particularly striking piece of jewelry: a small bit of red coral, with two clasped hands and a heart with a cross and anchor, a symbol of faith, hope and love. It allegedly came from the burnt farm. The driving force of the gang might have been the wife. Drinking and carousing followed each crime like a ritual, and fueled the gang members for the next deed. They received 15 years in prison and died behind bars. Their daughter got eight years, and the son, Ignatz, who was born in Metten in May, 1875, also got fifteen years.

On the night of September 30 and October 1, 1920, the Huber family had been slaughtered with an axe in Ebersberg. Ignatz was suspected by Chief Inspector Josef Rubner. At that time, he had reported the facts and pointed out that a woman had to be involved in the murder as a perpetrator.

On one hand of the deceased Huber woman, Rubner had discovered a strange woman's hair whose origin could not be ascertained. He also found at the scene strange, bloodstained hairpins. But the battered corpse of Mrs. Huber had made him think. Her head was terribly mutilated. From the very beginning Rubner had stated that only a hysterical woman could have killed her. The killers had also entered the house from the barn and the murder weapon belonged to the victims. He did not want to rule out the fact that a man was involved as well. This in turn could be Ignatz, since he had already served his 15 years in prison.

On his own time, Rubner studied the personal data and learned that Ignatz had already left the Kaisheim prison on May 6, 1917 and first moved to Rumfordstrasse with his widowed sister Anna, and later to Ebersberg. After learning that fact, Rubner pushed even harder that Ignatz should have to face the Ebersberger murder charges. What about the Hinterkaifeck killings? The quadruple and sixfold murders bore the same signatures. A man like Ignatz, whose life consisted only of criminal activity, was not beyond committing new crimes.

Ignatz was uneducated, never worked, lived only on robbing and stealing as taught by his parents. Inspector Rubner had seen the usefulness of punishment and knew inmates were not rehabilitated in prison. "Experience shows," he wrote, "that in the penitentiary they emerge no better. On the contrary, criminals seek new crimes after their release." One, like Ignatz, without a job, had no choice anyway, especially in the worst economic conditions. Times of progressive inflation had been even more destructive. He may have been alienated from the world after such a long separation from freedom and society.

Regarding Ignatz, Rubner continued to believe in his quilt and was not surprised at the man's pathetic life. "Work was never to his taste; he had a very luxurious life with his parents, as long as they did the raids." Since Ignatz, had been accustomed to crime from childhood onwards and he had returned to the criminal life, "It is not impossible that he took over his father's murder method."

As Rubner would discover later, Ignatz could not have committed the Ebersberg double murder in 1920. From October 1918 to the beginning of October 1921 he was serving another prison sentence in Straubing, At the time of the murders in Hinterkaifeck, however, he was a free man. He went straight for a time and worked on the Isar River deepening project between Puppling and Aumühle near Bad Tölz. Now the past caught up to him again as police investigated him and interrogated his associates, but found nothing.

On the day of the Hinterkaifeck murders Ignatz had worked on the Isar until evening. And the next morning he was back at the site from six o'clock in the morning. It would therefore take at least ten hours for the 140 kilometer round trip and without a motorbike or car that was impossible. Another good theory went into the trash can.

****

The mechanic, Albert Hofner was also briefly investigated when Georg Reingrubers realized that he had not been formality questioned in 1922. On May 7, 1925 the Neuburg prosecutor asked the Munich police on May 7, 1925 to investigate. Reingrubers was thus assigned along with Criminal Secretary, Kollmer because he knew the area around Hinterkaifeck the best.

Initially, Kollmer went to Pfaffenhofen an der Ilm. There he learned that the Ziegler machine factory, which sent the mechanic to Hinterkaifeck to fix the motor, had moved its factory to Reichertshausen, about six kilometers away. The new building was located outside the village, directly on the Munich-Ingolstadt railway line. The CEO, Johann Ziegler, was not there, but the bookkeeper offered to help. Kollmer requested a room where they could talk privately. Records of a service call to Hinterkaifeck no longer existed. Albert Hofner, who was the brother-in-law of the company owner, could only have received the order from the then factory manager, Lorenz Schmid. Hofner years later could not recall who gave him the repair order.

Johann Ziegler, who had arrived in the meantime, immediately realized that the order for the repair in Hinterkaifeck had been received by telephone. But who called and from where, he could not recall. He was surprised that, after such a long period of time, someone from Munich came to question his brother-in-law, whom he had employed as a new manager for his abilities alone and for no other reason. No nepotism there.

Ziegler offered the criminal secretary an empty office and a typewriter. The more he thought back, the more he remembered. The repair had been postponed several times because of bad weather. "Understand," he said to Kollmer, "Nobody wanted to go out with the bicycle at the time in the bad weather with the poor road conditions." This information should have already been in Schrobenhausen police files. An official had called the company the day after the discovery of the corpses and asked what mechanic had been sent to Hinterkaifeck.

Hofner, was amazed at the effort police made to discover information that was routine for him. He still had no clue he was a suspect. It was just an assignment of many, and even one that had been on going on for more than three years. It was not his first trip to Hinterkaifeck. He provided his personal details quite calmly.

Born on October 1, 1902 in Königsfeld, Pfaffenhofen District, he was the son of a blacksmith, Catholic, Bavarian and now living in Reichertshausen. He also described the day when he went to Hinterkaifeck, and how the cows mooing and the hoarse barking of a dog struck him as odd and that there was no one around with everything closed up, except for a barn door. Hofner was also not alarmed when Kollmer strangely asked him exactly what tools he had with him. Without the slightest suspicion he listed everything from the hammer to the pliers that were in his tool bag. Even the question of whether he had a pocketknife, did not alert him. He could not have known that there was a pocket knife found in the vicinity of the murder weapon unless he was the killer.

Kollmer even entered in the five-page report signed by Hofner: "I didn't have a pocket knife with me at that time, since most of the time I don't carry one with me at all."

The former operations manager, Lorenz Schmid, was also questioned by Kollmer. The 24-year-old car dealership owner in Pfaffenhofen, stated: "No, Hofner did not want to go to Hinterkaifeck at that time. It wasn't just the weather. Hofner had worked for the family once before and bitterly complained after his return that they were very unclean and that they were also very stingy. They had not even offered him a piece of dry bread for dinner."

The next day, Kollmer was with Lorenz Schlittenbauer in Gröbern. His daughters Maria and Victoria and son, Johann were also summoned by the criminal secretary. Schlittenbauer argued when he heard that Hofner was a suspect. "It is absolutely impossible that the mechanic had anything to do with the crime. Because he was at Hinterkaifeck on a Tuesday and on the Saturday before there were no signs of life. As proof he recalled the Sigl boy from Rachelsbach. He wanted to buy lard from Andreas Gruber on Sunday afternoon, but no one answered him. The boy told Schlittenbauer's son Johann, whom he met on the way back that, "They hid out on purpose. Maybe they could sell their lard somewhere else for more money."

Wangen's former mayor, Georg Gregers and Blasius Lebmeier from Oberkaifeck also agreed regarding the suspicion. "Hofner as a perpetrator is excluded completely."

Gregers provided Hofner with the very best testimony. "I've known him for a long time. This is a quiet and decent person."

Kollmer showed them the pocketknife, which had been found near the bodies in the barn under the hayloft floor. But no one knew to whom it belonged. In his final report to the prosecutor Kollmer summarized, "As far as the mechanic being the perpetrator is concerned, the testimony of persons questioned makes it perfectly clear that Hofner is completely eliminated as a suspect."

Police thought maybe the baker, Bärtl, who people were referred to as "crazy" could have committed the murders because he dated the new maid, Maria Baumgartner. A mysterious note had been sent to the Munich Public Prosecutor's Office suggesting the new maid might have been the motive. George Reingrubers tracked down her sister to explore that possibility. She had moved with her husband to Winterstrasse 3 in Munich.

Franziska had moved with her husband soon after a murder in Mühlried in Schrobenhausen to Munich. In the suburb of Giesing they bought the house on Winterstrasse 3. For the first time police learned something personal about the murdered maid.

"I certainly know", stated her sister, "that Maria had no love affairs." She had never given herself up to men, but put them off. A few years before her death Maria confided to her that she was pursued by a farmhand or hunter from Ecknach in Aichach with propositions. She did not recall a name. Maria had been very religious and diligently went to church. She never went to a dance hall. She lived with her mother for several years. It was only in recent years that she had been a maid for farmers. She made very little money. Most of the time she had only worked for room and board, which sometimes included clothing.

Franziska's husband, a 53-year-old worker who had been previously married, described his sister-in-law as being somewhat limited. Because of her shorter right leg, she had a limping gait, which some people made fun of. Maria had never mentioned name of Bärtl. The officials showed the couple two photographs of the Geisenfelder baker. But Franziska and her husband shook their heads that they did not recognize him.

During the night of February 26 to 27, 1926, a patrol car on Sonnenstrasse was stopped by a passerby. The man told the two officers that the Hinterkaifeck killer now and then stayed at Winterstrasse. All this he knew from a woman whose name he did not want to reveal. This witness believed that the owners of Winterstrasse 3 had contact with the killer. The owner reportedly said while drunk: "I've got something on my conscience that I must not tell anyone."

The night hawk informant, did not make a legit impression on Sgt. Johann Bruckmeier of the Schutzmannschaft 18th District police. The woman turned out to be the sister of Mary Baumgartner, Franziska. The "hint" alluded to by the note writer was based on neighborhood gossip, embellished by constant retelling.

Police checked the financial circumstances of the owners of Winterstrasse 3, but found nothing unusual. In June or July 1922, when inflation began to put them in the poor house, the couple sold their little house in Mühlried near Schrobenhausen and moved with only around 160,000 marks, which was very little money. Police only managed to learn that Franziska was very superstitious and she regularly read her tarot cards and firmly believed that there were three perpetrators at Hinterkaifeck. It seemed an odd coincidence that the murders occurred the same day the new maid arrived, but it was only happenstance.

Strange, but not as bizarre as the séances performed with the six skulls of the murder victims. Peter Leuschner, in his book, "Der Mordfall

Hinterkaifeck: Spuren eines mysteriösen Verbrechens",
described the sessions by Dr. Friedrich Sandner who
monitored the sessions suggested the idea. He was
specialist in nervous and mental disorders, who had
been director of an institution related to the
paranormal. He was a member a dueling fraternity with
Chief Inspector Ramer and invited his fraternity
brother, Ramer to the "Society for Scientific
Exploration, Occult Phenomena", founded only four
years earlier in Nuremberg.

In the 19th and early 20th centuries studying and
believing in the spiritual world was taken very
seriously. Many wealthy and influential people
belonged to such groups, so when the case went cold
the police gave the clairvoyant a chance.

Chief Prosecutor Ferdinand Renner allowed the
coroner, Dr. Aumüller, to bring the six prepared and
labeled calvariums to Nuremberg. In addition to the
package with the skulls, he had an envelope wrapped
in paper from the farm house, and the rope that had
been discovered at the scene of the crime. Which had
obviously been tied to a beam in the barn by unknown
persons. The clairvoyant said they needed some
personal possessions of the victims. Renner, along with
Dr. Böhm a veterinarian and a senior official of the
Nuremberg police, watched the medium who was
introduced to them only as a "Miss Jü."

The woman then performed, as most physics
do, with the usual theatrics and asking questions such
as, were the victims Catholic? She picked up each
package without opening it and mentioned that
vengeance was sought. In addition to the wrapped

skulls, police also brought other items like a wallet for her to read.

Miss Jü tossed out simple sentences like, "There is a curse on the family" and asked if one of the victims was named, Karla. She kept having a feeling there was a Karla involved. Andreas Gruber would not leave her alone as he was restless. She stated there were two women involved, one of them being a blonde.

To everyone watching it all sounded very confusing when words like "umbrella repairman" popped out. Afterward the medium briefly mentioned that she saw the maid the most clearly and she was the reason for the crime.

Dr. Böhm left the room with the large package. He returned with the skullcap of Maria Baumgartner and placed the package into the psychics' hands. Miss Jü held it over her head and spoke the completely disjointed words: "Ferry, Munich, Straubing, local railway." Then she suddenly asked the astonished prosecutor while pointing at the parcel with the maid's skull. "Is that from the maid?" And without waiting for an answer, the psychic added, "It is strange that she reveals so much." The psychic pointed to her right temple, then her face contorted and stated, "I feel a pain like the bone is injured."

The clairvoyant then described the escape route of the perpetrators as she crouched on the ground and hid her face in her hands. "Now I see a great city with a river and a bridge. Munich, Straubing and Landshut". The medium was exhausted and wanted to stop. The woman wanted to know from Renner, whether something personal from the maid was in the packet.

Renner nodded and she asked if she could open it. He told her she could, "I just don't think it will be pleasant."

Miss Ju needed a break and Dr. Böhm served her hot tea. She asked to continue the meeting in another room. Dr. Böhm suggested his study. There the psychic sat down on the heavy divan in the corner and pushed her face into a pillow.

"He that has done it, has no peace and it is because of the maid, and it shall come forth." Now she spoke more fluently and the words flowed: "The person is still very young, suffering terribly, I hear her pray, the dead have no rest." She called out the locations of Regensburg, Simmelsbach, Oberferrieden and Talheim. With a deep breath she added: "I think it ends there."

Josef Böhm disappeared into the other room and returned with the largest of the three packages, the skull of Andreas Gruber and handed it to the medium, Miss Jü. For some reason it was harder for her to see things clear now. She spelled out first an "E", then explained, "Through the E, I get Ebrach." Then Miss Jü's thoughts returned to Hinterkaifeck and she asked if groundwork had been done nearby. She described one of the perpetrators as about 30 years old, wearing something similar to military dress, who was known to Andreas Gruber.

After several minutes, Dr. Böhm stopped the session. Miss Jü had previously said: "I think we must stop; it seems to me to be futile." She had taken the package from the murder house unwrapped, but then she lay down again without a word. As it was already evening, Dr. Böhm wanted to continue the next day with a second medium.

At 8:50 in the morning they started again in the veterinarian's office. The second medium was called "Miss Bu" for the record. She was a young, cute girl gifted with psychic powers. In front of her on the table lay the skull of old Gruber, wrapped in brown packing paper. Miss Bu, also had a hard time getting into the mood with Andreas. Then the words came almost without interruption. The sentences seemed incoherent, incomprehensible.

Suddenly she described a man approaching a house and sneaking in. The characterization "hypocritical" and the words "He meets a second person" emerged. Then the medium described the murder weapon: "Something elongated, for beating, abominable, has some sharpness, more broad than narrow, but not so sharp." With great exertion she also portrayed the second man: "There is something shy about him, ugly laughter, younger, furrowed face, something piercing in the eyes, can be very distracting."

To the surprise of the group, the medium also saw two women, one younger and blonde and another who wanted to stop the crimes, but was pushed down and killed by one of the men. Despite all efforts, however, the medium did not succeed in describing the escape route of the perpetrators with more detail. Miss Bü saw a train station, railroad tracks on the left, many forests, meadows, a larger town where one of the two got off the train, a pointed church steeple and quite a few houses.

Josef Böhm requested that Miss Bü accompany him to the apartment of the other medium where he wanted to continue with both at the same time. It was an experiment Böhm wanted to try.

At 11:45 in the morning the two women sat around a table. Miss Jü, quickly grabbed the wrapped skull of Andreas Gruber, jumped up, and ran around the room excitedly. "I have to walk," she blurted, "I can't rest, I cannot sit down." Then she pressed the skull against her forehead. Both women spoke at the same time. Each of them stated that there was a blow that "went through and through".

Phrases erupted from them like "gaping wound and cursed", regarding the death of old man Gruber. The other medium also became increasingly ecstatic. Miss Jü laid on the ground, shouting loudly "damn gang". She had blotchy patches all over her face, suffered a sudden coughing attack and seemed to be suffocating. She stuttered something about Lower Bavaria. Her face changed abruptly, beaming she yelled out "Schwandorf! Now it's easier for me." The other medium also thought Schwandorf was where at least one of the perpetrators could be hiding.

On May 6, 1922, Miss Bü was in the office of Josef Böhm. The last session was three days earlier. She had more say about the story. "The old farmer was with me again, he gives me no peace, ask me again." Once again, the medium mentioned Schwandorf.

After half an hour, Dr. Böhm spread out photographs from the last Bavarian police journal before the young woman, but covered the names under the photographs. In the first two pictures she shook her head after studying them and stated the killer was not there. Josef Böhm then showed her photograph with the number 55. The medium enthusiastically said he was at the crime scene.

The number 55 was the baker, Joseph Bärtl, from Geisenfeid, near Ingolstadt, who escaped from the Günzburg mental hospital on July 4. He had since been sought by the police. Bohm then encouraged her to describe the second perpetrator.

Miss Bü thought carefully for a while then stated the man was in Nuremberg. The second man was large with red skin and had a suspicious appearance. Gruber had called him 'Red Joseph'. He has been an employee at Hinterkaifeck.

On May 5, Dr. Josef Böhm finished the first report then police director, Josef Ramer stated: "I would recommend that you check this out with skilled investigators especially in Schwandorf." Böhm suggested holding a meeting with the psychic in the murder house. Dr. Friedrich Sandner requested that Ramer check who was at the Hinterkaifeck house on St. Joseph's Day, March 19, as he could be the murderer.

Police should also determine whether any excavation work was done in the vicinity of Hinterkaifeck. Sandner hoped that Ramer could answer the following questions: "Were there workers who had to leave in the last 14 days, and had one of them been to Ebrach before? Or was there often a migrant trader there? Did anyone have a nickname that indicated a trade? Could it be ascertained which merchants the victims regularly sold their products?"

There were hundreds of other suspects police investigated either from circumstances, false confessions or tips from relatives who believed a family member or significant other was the perpetrator. The police did all due diligence in following every lead, no matter how unlikely. Even to the point of using psychics and checking out the information the gleaned from skull caps.

Chapter Twelve

Was Lorenz Schlittenbauer the Killer?

George Reingrubers retired on February 28, 1930 as head of the Munich Homicide Division. Until then, the Hinterkaifeck murder case focused on robbery as the motive. The reward of 100,000 marks for solving the crime brought in numerous tips to the police , but none led to sufficient evidence to convict any of the more than 100 people investigated since 1922.

After Reingrubers retired the homicide division of the Munich police department was taken over by Criminal Inspector Martin Riedmayr who questioned the motive for the crime in February 1931. He had been involved in the murder case in 1922 and thought too little attention was paid to the fact that Lorenz Schlittenbauer received money from Victoria Gabriel to finance acknowledgement of paternity of Joseph Gruber.

According to the facts, Andreas Gruber could possibly be the biological father of Joseph Gruber. In order to avoid another conviction of father and daughter because of incest, Victoria Gabriel started a relationship with Lorenz Schlittenbauer during the pregnancy in 1919. It was only later that Schlittenbauer recognized the connection, possibly by calculating the time of conception, when he then filed a complaint against Andreas Gruber for incest.

To avert legal proceedings, Victoria Gabriel turned to Schlittenbauer and asked him to acknowledge her paternity. Schlittenbauer had been offered the prospect of marrying Gabriel.

Riedmayr knew that Schlittenbauer received 5,000 marks from Victoria Gabriel on the third day after the birth of Joseph Gruber so that he could recognize paternity as Lorenz Schlittenbauer stated in his interrogation in March 1931. This was bribery. It was possible the money was given to Schlittenbauer so he could pay the child support payment and thus provide credibility to paternal recognition before the Guardianship Court. Schlittenbauer did not pay the alimony for Joseph Gruber out of pocket.

After recognition of paternity, Victoria Gabriel's promise of marriage was not kept as Andreas Gruber would not give permission. They also asked for the money back from Schlittenbauer. He was powerless to fight the situation. He was unable to disclose the agreement without - according to Riedmayr - "without throwing himself under the cart." Schlittenbauer may have tried to get at least some money, but this did not lead to the much given the Gabriel/Gruber family's miserly reputation.

Schlittenbauer must have been very resentful against the residents of Hinterkaifeck. The pot kept getting stirred when Schlittenbauer was asked why he hadn't yet married Victoria Gabriel.

The trigger for the crime was possibly an event not known up to then such as an argument with Victoria Gabriel, who, according to the police report, was probably the first to be killed. According to Riedmayr, this would make it understandable why the perpetrator's anger was also directed against the two-year-old Joseph Gruber. The prospects of convicting Lorenz Schlittenbauer were according to Riedmayr, "extremely slim", especially since the files do not provide any information concerning the whereabouts of the bribe money mentioned.

Investigations continued in other directions in the 1930s, but greed was still considered a motive. In a police report from 1948 it states: "Investigations in this regard were continuously carried out and extended to Lindau, Passau, Ingolstadt, Augsburg, etc.". According to the report, resumption of the investigations in 1948/52 in the Hinterkaifeck case reconsidered circumstantial evidence and in view of gold coins left behind at Hinterkaifeck points to "an act of revenge rather than a robbery".

At the end of the investigations in the Hinterkaifeck case (1952), the suspicions raised against the Gump brothers, in particular against the basket maker, Adolf Gump, combined the motives that Riedmayr considered probable with the original social motives suspected as early as the 1920s. The perpetrators could also be found among the roving traders, peddlers, basket makers, showmen or other "people wandering around in the gypsy manner" at the time.

Lorenz Schlittenbauer could not provide a sufficient alibi for the period of the crime. There was a possibility that Schlittenbauer was not on his property at the time in question, i.e., on the evening of March 31, 1922. The second wife of Schlittenbauer, Anna Dick, when asked whether her husband was at home the night of the murders, should have answered that he was not. Lorenz Schlittenbauer himself had replied: "I slept in the hay barn, so that I would not have to break in." What exactly he meant by this statement is uncertain.

When the bodies were discovered, Schlittenbauer was remarkably familiar with conditions at the crime scene. He accessed the property via the unlocked gate to the mechanical shed, then by pulling open the southern barn door, which was kept closed from the inside with a wooden rod. He would have been familiar with the buildings and layout of the farm and would know which gate would be easiest to enter.

Before entering the living quarters and before discovering the stroller in the bedroom, Schlittenbauer referred to Joseph Gruber to the other witnesses as "his boy", whom he had to look after as he might still be alive. However, since he charged Andreas Gruber with incest, he clearly rejected paternity. He did not believe he was the boy's father before March 31.

The main reason for recognition of paternity for Joseph Gruber on September 30, 1919, for Lorenz Schlittenbauer was probably sexual attraction and sexual favors from Victoria Gabriel at the end of 1918 which left a lasting impression on him. The marriage proposed by Victoria was seriously considered by Lorenz. The provision of 2000 marks, which covered the advance child support costs for Joseph Gruber, would not have created a sufficient incentive for recognition of paternity since he was wealthy.

Schlittenbauer made several changes to the crime scene and according to witness statements, Schlittenbauer did not try to stop people from touring the crime scene and destroying evidence until arrival of the first police officers. He ignored suggestions by witnesses to ensure that the crime scene was handed over to police without contaminating the scene.

Schlittenbauer offered some of the villagers arriving at the crime scene food supplies to eat on site. This led to police originally thinking that the perpetrators must have stayed on the property for several days cooking and consuming food. The killers may well have eaten food, but with the disruption of the scene it will never be known.

The investigating officers noticed the odd behavior of Schlittenbauer. He displayed excitement at the scene, talked constantly and made himself "important" in other ways. Today this behavior would be expected in a perpetrator. Schlittenbauer was well informed about domestic conditions of the murdered people and, as George Reingrubers noted in the report, "knows it best."

Schlittenbauer stated he owned the pickaxe in the barn. Gruber had stolen it and he wanted it back. After finding it, Schlittenbauer tried to obtain it. He told third parties that the perpetrator initially tried to bury the bodies in the barn, but the ground was too

179

hard. Maybe he tried using the pickaxe to dig. There are no references to this information in recorded witness statements - not even in the two statements by Schlittenbauer - nor in the police investigation files.

Contrary to witnesses Pöll and Sigl, Schlittenbauer testified that the hay rope was already hanging on the crossbar in the barn passage on the day it was found. He supported the idea presented by police regarding the robbery and murder theory and that the perpetrators used the rope hanging down in the barn passage to escape. "I was able to leave the property despite the doors and gates being locked inside". Since Schlittenbauer was on site every day in the days after the discovery up to the autopsy of the corpses, he was always informed about the current state of the investigation and any unanswered questions. The descriptions of anomalies in the initial investigation, which connected the act with a planned robbery all go back to information provided by Lorenz Schlittenbauer.

Schlittenbauer showed no empathy towards the victims when the crime was discovered or in later interrogations or conversations about the April 04.1922 discovery of the murders. The witnesses Pöll and Sigl found it disturbing, that Schlittenbauer repositioned the corpses by hand in order to be able to see the dead better.

Schlittenbauer conducted routine business immediately after the bodies were found and before the arrival of the first police officers in taking care of the livestock on Hinterkaifeck. Witnesses reported that immediate feeding was not necessary to control the behavior of the animals. It was almost as if he expected to inherit the property.

The unlocking of the front door from the inside, as reported by witnesses, cannot in every case be regarded as an indication of Lorenz Schlittenbauer's guilt. It was assumed that there was only one key for Hinterkaifeck as even Schlittenbauer believed. Surely, Cecilia and Victoria had keys. Gruber said he lost a key, but did not mean there were no others. Missing a key would also be cause for alarm with the amount of people coming and going for work or business. Anyone might have taken one.

According to the case information available, the perpetrator visited the property several times up to the day of discovery of the crime. He most likely left the building through a door that could be locked. On April 4 when the bodies were found, with the exception of the courtyard gate that could not be locked, all entrances to the property were secure.

Schlittenbauer suffered from asthma, which has been reported several times but cannot be taken as evidence against him being the killer. It could be assumed that he would not have laid in hay if suffering from asthma, but as cold as the weather was at the time of the crime, he may not have been suffering much from it or allergies. Police also did not believe Lorenz could have had enough stamina to kill six people.

Inspector Reingrubers excluded Lorenz Schlittenbauer from the group of suspects two days after finding the corpses due to lack of a motive for the crime. His opinion was based on information provided by the mayor of Wangen. He did state that Schlittenbauer had "shown a little excited behavior" at the crime scene, talked a lot and made himself "important in other ways", but attributed this to the fact his own child, the 2 ½ years old Joseph Gruber was among the victims. Mayor Gregers believed Schlittenbauer gave "honest testimony" shortly after the crime became known.

In the report of the public prosecutor, Ferdinand Renner, of April 10, 1922, Reingrubers's assessment of the motive was followed by other officers. He stated, "Schlittenbauer, was described as suspicious himself, but is generally described as a somewhat strange, but harmless, good-natured and always helpful person and is himself willing, a motive is not recognizable".

Renner's successor, Richard Pielmayer reported in 1926, that Schlittenbauer was out of the question as a perpetrator because of his personality, and he, like the public prosecutor, made reference to the recorded statement that acknowledgment of paternity was not financially a motive. Schlittenbauer's interrogation did not take place until 1931. According to the files, the investigative work of detectives in 1922 concentrated increasingly on the Munich urban area and not on local populations.

A follow-up of the suspicious facts and critical evidence collected up to that point in 1931 was ignored in favor of an evaluation of the suspect's personality. Lorenz Schlittenbauer was questioned on March 30, 1931 years after the incident and it is well known that criminals are less likely to confess the more time passes. Recollections fade even with the innocent.

Police never examined whether the crime might have a religious motive either. Schlittenbauer when discussing marriage to Victoria with her father stated that Andreas had to lay off sexual relations with his daughter after the marriage. He was going to set her on the right path and redeem her. The murder of the two children was horrendous. One could fathom that Schlittenbauer would blame Victoria and her parents for the unholy household, but making the children pay is hard to understand. The girl could identify him, which could be why he killed her, but bashing the skull in of a toddler was not necessary unless he thought little Joseph was a demon child that needed to be erased.

The villagers in the Gröbern community, were cautious about expressing opinions against Schlittenbauer for fear of being troublemakers. this applies to witness, Jakob Sigl, who later accused Lorenz Schlittenbauer of the crime and who, after several threats against him, moved to Schiltberg near Aichach in 1933. The witness, Wenzeslaus Bley, from Schrobenhausen claimed that Jakob Sigl told him that witnesses did not tell the truth during the investigations out of fear of Lorenz Schlittenbauer.

As mentioned earlier, the Munich police probably never received all information relevant to the crime from Gröbern villagers. With the exception of Jakob Sigl, the witnesses residing in Gröbern only suspect people who do not belong to the village community, the old "things like that don't happen here" belief.

Eventually other people who do not belong to the village community come under suspicion, including the brothers of Karl Gabriel. The need to keep the village community united stifled accusations against Schlittenbauer for years after the offense. The later election of Johann Schlittenbauer as town leader of Gröbern proves the desire for solidarity and lack of conflict, despite suspicions.

The offense was triggered by a child support and paternity dispute over Joseph Gruber, after the second filing of incest charges, which ended in May 1920 with Victoria Gabriel and Andreas Gruber's acquittal. Lorenz Schlittenbauer initially had no opportunity to contest obligations entered into with Joseph Gruber's recognition of paternity in September 1919.

Schlittenbauer married Anna Dick, who had a son from a previous marriage and whose adoption was planned and a prerequisite for marriage. She was almost 18 years younger than Lorenz. He appealed to Victoria Gabriel regarding paternal child support. Since the previous marriage agreements between them had been denied, he wanted Victoria to explain to the guardianship court that he was not the father of little Joseph, but some other man. In this way, Schlittenbauer hoped to reverse inheritance-related issues resulting from acknowledgment of paternity for his son Johann and his adoptive son, Joseph Dick.

Victoria Gabriel was already unwilling to make such a declaration due to the fact that Schlittenbauer filed a complaint against her and her father on September 10th, 1919 and October 8th, 1919 for incest. In addition, she would again expose herself and her father to the danger of being charged with a crime against morality. It was obvious that she was offering Schlittenbauer money to prevent further advances by him. Since Schlittenbauer was wealthy, it was not a great plan.

In expectation of their first child together with his second wife Anna, Lorenz Schlittenbauer was no longer willing to accept the economic disadvantages and resulting internal family burden for Joseph Gruber due to the parental recognition. He made several attempts at the beginning of 1922 to confront Victoria Gabriel on the paternity matter. Gabriel avoided Schlittenbauer after an argument on the street.

In order to counter the growing pressure from Schlittenbauer, Victoria Gabriel demanded return of the money lent to Schlittenbauer for acknowledgment of paternity based of a promissory note or a comparable agreement. It would provide evidence of the transaction, which would lead Schlittenbauer, as a public official, to be suspected of accepting the money from Victoria Gabriel due to financial need. After Anna Schlittenbauer gave birth in early March the child support amount set at 1,800 marks would go against Schlittenbauer, who could not disclose the original agreement that led to the paternal recognition without exposing himself to a bribery charge.

Schlittenbauer most likely was not the father of little Joseph, but Andreas Gruber. Victoria Gabriel was guilt ridden and ashamed over the matter and with Schlittenbauer backing out of the agreement she placed the 700 gold marks in the confessional of the Waidhofen parish church at the beginning of March 1922

The conflict between the families escalated with the death of Schlittenbauer's youngest daughter, who died of whooping cough on March 26, 1922 at the age of just a few weeks and was buried on March 30, 1922. On the evening of March 31, 1922 Schlittenbauer, emotionally upset after the death of his daughter - decided to confront Victoria Gabriel at Hinterkaifeck, perhaps to retrieve the agreement, since it appeared that the killer searched through personal papers at the crime scene. His copy of the contract probably burnt in the house fire on his property.

Sometime after 8:00 p.m., Schlittenbauer approached Hinterkaifeck from the forest side in the direction of Hexenholz (Witches Wood) to the south. The distance to the property was only 165 feet from there, which was covered in darkness over an open field. He probably practiced or attempted entering the farm courtyard for several days without going through with the plan to confront Victoria. Gruber had reported seeing someone standing at the edge of the forest, but did not recognize him.

Schlittenbauer entered the barn passage through the courtyard gate, which is only locked with a piece of wood wedged between the floor and the door.

There he grabbed the pickaxe as it was handy and broke into the barn by violently ripping open the southern barn door. Though it was hard to hear voices in the barn from the living area, it is questionable that the residents could not hear that type of racket. He could have picked the lock to enter the barn through the north gate and then retrieved the pickaxe in the barn. The farm dog, which was on a leash in the barn in the evenings, may have barked at the intruder, but as noises in the barn demonstrably could not be heard from the living quarters, the residents were not warned. One would then ask, why post a dog outside if his barking could not be heard? The dog may have seen Schlittenbauer often enough that he recognized him and was not alarmed.

As the closest neighbor, Schlittenbauer was familiar with the daily routine at Hinterkaifeck. He knew that Victoria Gabriel was responsible for checking the barns in the evening. Schlittenbauer waited for her barn check in the barn in order to be able to hide in the attic or to escape from the building, if Victoria Gabriel entered the barn or if several residents decided to do the inspection. The intruder used a flashlight to orient himself in the dark barn. In order to prevent Gabriel from leaving the barn after a short visual inspection, Schlittenbauer led a cow out of the feed room into the barn and tied it up there. He left the door between the feed room and the barn open so that noises from the livestock could be heard from the barn.

Victoria Gabriel left the kitchen around 9 p.m., passed the cellar anteroom and opened the door to the feed room and noticed the open door to the barn. She attached the kerosene lamp to a wall bracket in the feed room and walked towards the barn to bring the rambling single cow back into the barn.

At this point Schlittenbauer may have tried to have a conversation with Victoria that did not go well. Either out of panic or anger he then struck her with the mattock on the right side of her head. He may have been drunk, which loosened his inhibitions. The perpetrator probably strangled Victoria Gabriel after inflicting several blows with the mattock.

While Schlittenbauer was still bending over Victoria Gabriel, who no longer showed any sign of life, Cecilia Gruber entered the barn to check on her daughter. Believing that Victoria Gabriel was in the barn, she walked towards the open barn door. Upon entering the barn, Cecilia Gruber saw Victoria lying on the ground and would naturally cry for help. The intruder choked Cecilia Gruber to prevent her from screaming. He pulled her to the ground and hit the woman's head several times with the mattock.

  The perpetrator, assuming that the other two residents, Andreas Gruber and Cecilia Gabriel would searching for Victoria, waited with the mattock ready, with his back to the western wall of the barn. With the blunt side of the mattock toward the barn door, he struck the forehead and right side of the head of people entering the barn. The seven-year-old Cecilia Gabriel was thrown to the ground by the force of the first blow. The next blow hit as the girl was falling or already lying on the ground, below the chin and caused a transverse neck wound, which only led to death several hours later.

  After the attack on Cecilia Gabriel, Schlittenbauer entered the residential area of the building. At this point he did not know that the new maid, Maria Baumgartner, arrived at Hinterkaifeck a few hours ago. He must have assumed that only the toddler was in the house. The fact that the mattock was taken into the residential wing shows there was intent to kill the 2-year-old Joseph Gruber.

  The perpetrator remained in the kitchen for a short time when he noticed a person in the maid's room. He carefully opened the ajar door to the maid's room and slammed the mattock into Maria

Baumgartner's head as she was about to unpack her bag and then turned toward the opening door.

From the maid's room, Schlittenbauer went into Victoria Gabriel's bedroom. He stopped in front of the stroller and struck the face of the sleeping Joseph Gruber with the blunt side of the mattock through the stroller cover. The child was killed in one blow.

In Victoria Gabriel's bedroom, Schlittenbauer searched in drawers and through notes and legal papers for a contract or promissory note, which he finally found in Victoria Gabriel's wallet. The document was probably a monetary obligation related to paternity recognition for Joseph Gruber at the expense of Lorenz Schlittenbauer.

In order not to have to leave the property with the murder weapon, the killer went from the bedroom via the stairs in the hallway to the attic He did the blood-stained mattock in the false floor above the kitchen. However, the six victims were not covered immediately after the crime.

The killing of all the residents took about 1 hour. Another 1-2 hours were needed to search the bedroom and hide the mattock, so that Schlittenbauer checked the crime scene around 11:30 p.m. and left. He blocked all entrances; including the southern barn door, which was secured from the inside with a wooden pole that may have been temporarily attached after the forced break-in. The perpetrator left the building through an entrance that can be locked from the outside.

With the intent to further cover up the crime, the killer returned several times between March 31 and on April 4, 1922. A longer stay on Hinterkaifeck was too risky for the perpetrator and he had his own farming obligations. He only undertook such work as milking and watering livestock to prevent the crime from being discovered through excessive protesting of the animals. The animals were not adequately fed during this time, only the minimum to keep them quiet. Since the 2-year-old calf was one of the weaker animals, Schlittenbauer did not bring the animal back into the barn, but simply untied it. When the witness, Andreas Schwaiger, arrived, the cow was still walking around the barn eating the hay stored there.

When Schlittenbauer returned to the property the day after the crime on Saturday, April 1st, 1922, he planned to bury the corpses in the barn. Since excavation was not possible due to the frozen barn floor, the corpses lying near the barn door were placed on top of each other to be temporarily covered with hay. the killer placed a door panel on the haystack for additional cover. Was there symbolization or staging in stacking the corpses in the barn? Or did the killer really plan to bury the bodies and placed them there out of convenience?

Assuming that the perpetrator approached the property after dark in the first few days after the crime, a visit by the killer on the morning of April 4, 1922 indicated that the cattle were not being looked after regularly. The last time was on the late evening of April 2nd, 1922 and that, from the perpetrator's point of view, there was a risk of the crime being discovered by the animals becoming audibly restless in the surrounding fields. It can be assumed that Schlittenbauer was at Hinterkaifeck on Saturday (April 1st), Sunday (April 2nd) and Tuesday (April 4th).

Since on April 4, Schlittenbauer approached the property from the forest side, he initially missed the presence of the mechanic Albert Hofner. Schlittenbauer only noticed the mechanic when he was sitting behind the house on his bicycle and drew attention to himself by whistling loudly and later doing his work in the engine shed while singing and whistling. This must have caused sheer panic in Schlittenbauer.

To prevent the mechanic from entering the yard and looking for the residents, Schlittenbauer tied the yard dog to the front door. This was intended to create the impression that the farm residents were only temporarily out of the house and left the dog to guard the property.

While the mechanic Hofner repaired the engine, Schlittenbauer was inside the house, possibly in the attic of the house since Hofner could look through one of the windows again and see him. It was only when Hofner finished his work around 2:30 p.m. and drove off on his bike in the direction of Gröbern that Schlittenbauer was able to leave the property unnoticed. The perpetrator brought the farm dog back into the barn, locked all doors and left the property in the direction of the nearby forest.

Allegedly, Lorenz Schlittenbauer stated on his deathbed in 1941 that he had nothing to do with the six murders at Hinterkaifeck. The pastor of Waidhofen at that time, Johann Baptist Bumiller (Born 09/14/1899, Died 09/03/1965) gave the dying man the Last Rites and was present when the final words were spoken. The pastor wrote a report in a church newspaper in

1941 stating that "A dying person does not lie". The family never saw the article.

The previous description of the crime is a commonly assumed chronology of the murders and does seem logical. There have been other multiple murders that occurred in one location with just one perpetrator, so the method is not unknown. Schlittenbauer's wife, Anna could have lied about the number of times he was gone. She had to have noticed her husband being absent at night and just alibied him.

With the close knit Gröbern community it is questionable that Schlittenbauer had not heard about the new maid being hired since Victoria made the trip out of town to inquire about one. He seems to have been aware of everything else the family did. Whether or not he knew about Maria by the time he had killed four people, he was probably so enraged that she was just one more outlet. Smashing the baby in the face indicated that he saw the child as a product of incest and not his own son. Anger over Victoria's offer of marriage and then refusal provoked fury and jealousy. She would rather have sex with her father than him. Then when his first child with his new wife died shortly after birth, it seemed like a smack in the face. Schlittenbauer wanted the paperwork evidence where he admitted paternity of the child, Joseph Gruber to destroy it.

Why didn't he just demand the paper back? Maybe he did and Victoria refused. Clearly, she did not believe Schlittenbauer was the father either as she made a large donation to the church to ease her conscious. Andreas Gruber was furious when he discovered that his daughter had given the church the large sum and beat her, prompting her to run into the woods.

In December 1933 police learned of a strange incident on February 3, 1924 in Brunnen. A woman named Walburga K. had appeared at the Schrobenhausen SA office of the special commissar in Wiedmann. She had sat next to Lorenz Schlittenbauer at the funeral dinner. While eating she started chatting about Hinterkaifeck - without mentioning the name. After a few sentences Schlittenbauer joined the conversation. "I am surprised," she said to him, "that so many clever gentlemen sit in judgment and yet nothing comes of it." And then she speculated that someone must have fed the cattle, even the sows, because otherwise they would have eaten the stored potatoes.

Schlittenbauer allegedly replied: "If everyone was as clever as you, they would have caught him already. But they did not catch him that way." He pulled his eyelids all the way up and stuck his tongue out. Locals had described Lorenz as a strange, but harmless guy.

When she mentioned the paternity matter, he stated: "I'll be the father, but you'll have to atone for it." Then he blurted: "He who killed them did not commit murder, but exterminated incest." During the conversation, Schlittenbauer suddenly became so excited that he threw the knife his wife had given him to eat dinner at the wall. With such behavior and remarks it isn't hard to understand why he was a prime suspect. It has caused his family much misery over the years.

One local family would like to end the rumors about Hinterkaifeck. "It never ends, never a rest," complained Regina Weichselbaumer. The 85-year-old is the daughter of Lorenz Schlittenbauer, the farmer whom many locals and other supposed experts believe was the murderer.

His sons, Lorenz and Alois, were most affected. Even as a young apprentice carpenter, Alois was rejected by a customer: "I can't let him in here, I don't want to see him." Regina was also often hurt as a girl: "We don't want to be killed!", people would say. "Once the pastor offered to accompany us home after school," reported Regina Weichselbaumer. "On the way he then tried to sound us out inconspicuously."

In 1949, the Schlittenbauer's were attacked and robbed. Their neighbor was only poisoned: "That was revenge for Hinterkaifeck." Alois Schlittenbauer is still annoyed today when he goes to the local inn in the village of Baar-Ebenhausen to play cards and is greeted by some with the words "Ah, there comes the son of the Hinterkaifeck murderer".

Lorenz Schlittenbauer knew how much his children had to suffer because of him. "Sometimes he cried and said, I don't know why no one believes me," son Alois stated. He is certain that his father was not the murderer: "He was 30 percent disabled by the war, had no teeth and severe asthma." His father had coughed day in and day out, "because of the wheezing he couldn't do any hard work, how was he supposed to have killed six people?" Schlittenbauer's asthma could have been severe and may have been caused by exposure to mustard gas during combat.

"Father always told us that the affair with Victoria was the only mistake in his life," reports daughter Regina. "We stood around his deathbed and he said he had nothing to do with it," asserts Lorenz junior. Pastor Hans Bumiller was there and even wrote in a church newspaper in 1942 "that he believes him because the dying don't lie".

Josef Plöckl, the former mayor of Waidhofen, is nevertheless certain: "It wasn't Schlittenbauer." He knew another name - some old people might have said it when they were dying, but Plöckl does not want to reveal this name: "It is very sensitive, the descendants are still alive." There are questions regarding Schlittenbauer's guilt and he did deny the murders on his death bed in 1965, not that some people do not lie even at the end.

In 2007 the police academy in Fürstenfeldbruck evaluated the old criminal files using the latest investigation methods. The fifteen students discovered interesting insights, but would not reveal which perpetrator they suspected. Many assume it was Schlittenbauer and police won't reveal the name due to living descendants in the area. The almost 200-page work is considered "confidential classified information for official use only". Most seem to believe he was the killer, but there is one interesting alternative theory.

Chapter Thirteen

Andreas Gruber

The possibility that Andreas Gruber might have been a family annihilator occurred to this author, but since he was also killed it had to be an outsider, right? Not according to the writer, Adolph J. Koppel in his nonfiction book, "Der Gruber War's: Lückenlose Aufklärung Mordfall Hinterkaifeck. German" officials dismiss his theory; however, Koppel does provide answers to some questions with the idea that Andreas murdered his family.

Koppel contends that Gruber used three tools as weapons; the mattock, pocket knife and the iron band, which police considered as well. The mattock was found in the attic floor along with the knife and iron band. Officials disregarded the knife at the time,

196

but Koppel thinks Gruber used it to cut Cilli's throat since he carried one as did many farmers. Koppel also has an interesting observation about the purpose of the homemade mattock. Gruber kept pigs and he designed the tool to first stun the animal and then cut its throat. This would be similar to kosher butchering where the animal is spared the trauma, which ruins the meat. This would explain the "unprofessional" construction that allowed the screw to stick out from both sides of the handle, which produced the star-shaped wounds.

The killer was good at using the tool and could have disabled his victims quickly and then used the flat end of the tool to bash their skulls. Since Gruber had experience killing pigs with it, he could have taken people out with little trouble. As Koppel points out, it would take skill and practice to just penetrate the brain enough to kill, but an angry person could easily crack the skull and do massive damage to the skull.

Andreas was a cruel man who had little regard for his family, neighbors or employees. He had used tools as weapons against people in the past such as pitchforks and shovels. He kept his children in the cellar as punishment and at least one died for sure, Sophie. The fate of the others is unknown, but they are assumed dead.

His anger towards his daughter Victoria over wanting other men was a catalyst for disaster. Probably both of her children were fathered by Andreas and he only allowed her contact with Lorenz and Karl due to being pregnant and facing shame for being unwed. Karl did marry her and regretted doing so. As she told Schlittenbauer, "It's the better thing that I am pregnant by my father, otherwise he would kill me."

Koppel makes some other observations that should not be dismissed. The strangling of Victoria was personal and the little girl dying last was not an accident. Gruber wanted to rape her, which does explain why she was half naked and not killed immediately. After seeing her mother and grandmother murdered, however, the child would have been horrified and fought him off. Koppel thinks the child screamed and Gruber hit her mouth with the iron band to shut her up. By this time, he was furious and went into the house to kill the maid and exterminate the toddler.

Gruber could have also cleaned up much of the blood since only a few drops were found. Being familiar with slaughtering pigs he would also be experienced in removing blood and guts. As Schlittenbauer suggested, the killer may have tried to bury the bodies in the barn, but the ground was frozen.

Stashing the weapons in the attic floor does indicate someone very familiar with the house. As Koppel states, the space was large enough to hold the mattock and the killer knew that under the floor boards such a place existed. Lorenz could have figured it out if he had indeed spent much time in the attic, but it is equally plausible that Gruber could have stayed in the attic after the deed too afraid to leave the house.

Lorenz Schlittenbauer's statement: "This is my mattock. I recognize it, so it was there on the farm the whole time." By this he meant that his neighbors should finally realize that he could not have been the murderer, because he did not know where the murder weapon was hidden. If he had been the murderer, he would certainly not have hidden his tool in the house where everyone was slain

Koppel believes that Gruber tripped and fell on the mattock in the barn near the feeding trough, causing the wound to his face and carotid artery, He then lay there and bled out.

The calendar displaying the date of April 1, 1922 suggests to Koppel that someone in the family must have been alive that morning as it was a "sacred" duty of the head of the family to perform that ritual. Gruber could have torn it off after midnight or even before, maybe even when passing by it to kill the maid. He has a point. Why would a murderer bother to update the calendar?

The issue of the dog not being killed right off is a puzzle too if a stranger or outsider committed the crimes. The dog would not have been concerned about Gruber being in the barn or anywhere else, but then why was the Spitz hit? It could be that the screams of the little girl alerted the dog prompting a blow from the mattock. If Gruber was flustered after killing the girl he may not have hit the dog in the right place to kill it.

The timing of the murders was also poor due to the fact that neighbors in the surrounding farms would not have been asleep nor were the victims. Something must have agitated Gruber and set him off, since waiting for the family to retire would have been the better option. Perhaps the wife and daughter had reached a breaking point and spoke their minds? It could explain why the maid had not unpacked her things or why they had not had dinner.

Killers usually do not hang around after committing crimes. If Schlittenbauer had killed them, why would he risk returning to the scene to feed animals? Why not just let the bodies be discovered? So what if the animals raised a ruckus? Let someone else discover the horror. The stories about the family being watched were hearsay as well as the footprints. Koppel states that Gruber moved the roof tiles to watch for police since he had nowhere else to go. The murders were probably not planned, but the results of rage brought on by some incident. Gruber found himself stranded.

Andreas staying in the attic also explains why feces was discovered near one of the hay bales and the smoked meat being eaten. The two indentions in the piles of hay could have been where Gruber slept as his bed was still made up. He also would have baked bread without being concerned and could have been who was seen outside near the oven. At that time no one knew about the murders.

Before March 31st, Andreas had supposedly told neighbors that they heard footsteps in the attic, but he had gone upstairs with his shotgun and found no one and nothing unusual. There was nowhere for an intruder to hide in the open attic. The presence of the rope in the hayloft is questioned by Koppel as it was not mentioned by Gruber, as it should have been if a stranger had placed it there. It is odd that police stated the rope was not there the first time they searched. The rope could have been used to haul hay up to the loft, but if so, why wasn't it discovered when police searched? Of course, the barn and attic were not searched right away, so the scene was contaminated.

Gruber as the killer also explains why coins, bank bonds and jewelry were left behind. The house was also not ransacked except for Victoria's closet. Even if Gruber was the killer, Schlittenbauer could still have searched for the paternity paper after discovering the bodies and taken the paper money.

Gruber was found in his night clothes, which police thought could mean that the killer removed the bloody clothes and washed them in hot water and then burned Cazillia's and Cilli's clothes in the oven to cover up the crime. This is plausible as the oven or wash house was near the road. According to the witness, Michael Plöckl, the air stank of burnt rags on the evening of April 1, 1922. The oven was used during the day for baking bread and doing the laundry and not at night, but it does not mean that a panicked killer would not have tried destroying evidence in that manner. Koppel suggests that Gruber hung up the wet laundry in the living area to dry, which was why he was found in his underwear.

When the killer could not bury the bodies due to frozen ground, he covered them up with hay and an old door. If an outsider committed the crimes why bother trying to bury them or hide them? A stranger or Schlittenbauer could simply flee the scene and not come back. Covering the corpses indicates a personal relationship with the dead. "The killer struck Victoria 9 times and his wife Cecilia 8 times. This means that an "overkill" took place. Andreas Gruber couldn't cope with the fact that his daughter wanted to leave him. He vented his hate, frustration, and anger on her and the others."

It does not make sense that Schlittenbauer hid a tool that belonged to him, but was stolen and modified by Gruber. Lorenz kept it covered up in the field to avoid carrying it home very night. Gruber had found it and taken it, used it to kill and then hid it in the attic.

Plus, the pocket knife was usually kept in Gruber's pants pocket, so how would Schlittenbauer even get it?

"Completely illogical and incomprehensible actions for an outsider: No one comes to a farm without a weapon in order to then kill 4 adults and 2 children with an unfamiliar tool with a sophisticated striking technique, then hides the murder weapon(s) with considerable effort, high risk combined with a lot of time in strange house, only to then flee". Koppel observes.

So, if Schlittenbauer only discovered the murders why did he not leave and call police? Koppel states it was because he would be a prime suspect since locals knew he did not get along with Gruber and he had admitted being the father of Joseph and did not marry Victoria. It was known that Gruber denied her permission to marry him, so Schlittenbauer had motive.

There is the possibility that Lorenz discovered the bodies before April 4, 1922. Wonder if he found Gruber wounded and still clinging to life on April 1st ? Did he watch him bleed out or speed up the process? Schlittenbauer was very familiar with the crime scene when he discovered the bodies with his neighbors. Gruber could have already hidden the murder weapons in the attic leaving the pickaxe in the feed room available for Lorenz to finish Gruber off. After seeing what carnage the man caused, it is understandable why Schlittenbauer would kill him.

The eyewitness, Michael Plöckl, testified that he had seen Lorenz Schlittenbauer with a battery-powered flashlight on the evening of April 1, 1922 at the bakery at Hinterkaifeck. If Lorenz had discovered

202

the bodies shortly after the murders, he could have been the one destroying evidence. It is hard to fathom how a man with asthma could have had the ability to kill that many people, which is one reason police dismissed him as a suspect. It would not stop him from cleaning up, however.

Why did he go to Hinterkaifeck then? The rumors about the family being watched might have been true. It could have been Lorenz studying them from the forest. Even though he had remarried, it was clear that Schlittenbauer had a passion for Victoria. With his first child with Anna Dick dying, it must have seemed like the last straw. Maybe he planned to kill Gruber and walked into the aftermath or heard Cilli scream?

Whoever killed the Hinterkaifeck residents was familiar with their habits and the layout of the farm and buildings. It is unfortunate that fingerprints were not taken and the house destroyed. It would be interesting if blood samples could be analyzed from the murder weapons and compared with Schlittenbaur's decedents. It could rule Lorenz out as the murderer or confirm suspicions.

Chapter Fourteen

Conclusion

Hundreds of suspects were questioned over decades during investigations of the homicides at the Hinterkaifeck farm. There were many who might have committed the crimes as the Grubers hired roving farm hands and were generally not well liked by employees or local residents of Gröbern.

Many were questioned solely based on accusations such as Kasper Wendelin from Waidhofen and Andreas Thaler (senior) of Kaifeck being the Hinterkaifeck killers. The reason given by the witness is the fact that Andreas Kaspar, son of Wendelin Kaspar and married to a daughter of Thaler, built a house before the murder, but had to stop construction due to lack of money. Thaler wanted to take out a loan, but he would have had to raise a surety. Shortly after the murder, Thaler no longer needed a guarantee and the house could continue to be built, which was noticed at the time. Furthermore, the witness had heard

204

that Wendelin and Thaler were said to have paid the bricklayers and carpenters with gold after the murders. This was gleaned from a letter from the Schrobenhausen Police Station to the chief prosecutor at the Augsburg Regional Court in Schrobenhausen, January 3rd, 1934. The 66-year-old trader Maria Grassl from Schrobenhausen, supposedly said to the wife of the butcher, Kaspar Wendelin from Waidhofen, that Wendelin was rumored to be have committed murders in Hinterkaifeck. Police dismissed him as a suspect.

Employees found the Gruber family stingy, dirty and locals disapproved of the way Andreas Gruber treated his wife and children. The Grubers would not have won any popularity contests, especially with incest charges among their faults and child abuse. But who really had motive and opportunity to kill them?

Lorenz Schlittenbauer has long been a prime suspect and for many he was guilty of the murders. He certainly had motive and was familiar with the property. He wanted to marry Victoria, who frustrated him with marriage proposals and then denials. Locals assumed he was the father of the toddler, Joseph, so when he did not marry her, the villagers made their disgust known. Jealousy and humiliation could have pushed him too far, but far enough to butcher the entire family and the maid? He might have seen the boy as a product of the grandfather, thus needing eliminated. Why would Lorenz have been so mad at Cecilia Gruber or the little girl? Witnesses stated that Schlittenbauer had little contact with the women at the farm when he visited, only dealing with Andreas. The murders appear much too personal for a man who was jilted and wanted a legal document returned.

Of course, sometimes human beings do not need a rational explanation for the cruel acts they commit. We cannot really know the personalities of the people involved or exactly what transpired to flame emotions over one hundred years ago.

What about a second perpetrator? Could Paul Mueller have worked on the farm and became acquainted with Schlittenbauer? The crime was similar to ones he was suspected of committing in America. He was a carpenter, so he could have been hired for his skills in constructing the new barn. His unkept and creepy appearance probably would not have put Gruber off if he needed the labor. Surely though, he would have been remembered by locals, unless Mueller never went to town. He also preferred to kill his victims while asleep.

The killer was very familiar with the farm and buildings, inside and out. The brutality inflicted on the victims suggests rage and covering up the bodies can indicate remorse or a twisted respect for the dead. The idea that Andreas Gruber committed the murders should not be dismissed. The maid was probably collateral damage, but since the Grubers knew she was coming there must have been some additional event that sparked the crime. Andreas was already angry over his daughter giving so much money to the church; did she have plans to leave and her father figured it out? The old pervert would not let her marry anyone after Karl Gabriel, so Andreas certainly would not let her leave him. The farm belonged to her, was he afraid that he would be the one thrown out? Even though he once threatened to leave if Schlittenbauer married Victoria it was probably just that; an empty threat.

Gruber could have killed them before the maid showed up. He must have known Victoria went out of town to ensure the maid's employment. What could have happened that it was worth killing a stranger along with the family?

Did Schlittenbauer visit the farm prior to April 4, when the crime was discovered? According to witnesses he was a tour guide at the crime scene and was not bothered by the gore nor was he surprised. His wife, Anna, had lied about his whereabouts before, so she was not an alibi to rely on. If Lorenz was there just after the murders, what was he doing there? Was he an accomplice to the murders and showed up to check to see if they had indeed been killed? The actual killer could have been long gone.

If the crime had occurred prior to Schlittenbauer marrying Anna Dick, he would have had a good motive to kill Andreas Gruber. As Victoria's husband he would be owner of Hinterkaifeck, but Lorenz was already married. It would not have been necessary to murder the other five people either. Gruber could have been killed in the barn and Lorenz could have returned home with his wife to alibi him.

Schlittenbauer may have been a stalker that could not give up on Victoria, even with a new wife. It was common knowledge that Gruber beat his wife and daughter, so it would not be a stretch that Lorenz would sneak around watching out for her. With the death of his first child with Anna, Lorenz was probably emotionally frustrated and demoralized. If he had found Andreas Gruber still alive after slaughtering his family, Schlittenbauer might have finished him off and then went to search for the paternity document.

How likely is it that Schlittenbauer knew about the hiding place in the attic? If he had killed everyone, why would he hide tools used to murder that Gruber possessed? It is difficult to imagine that Lorenz would murder the two children, unless he believed they would recognize him or he was simply in a rage and could not stop.

It is not so difficult to imagine that Gruber could kill the two children, however. Joseph and Cilli were evidence of his sexual crimes, daily reminders to everyone that he did disgusting things with his adult daughter, which probably started long before puberty. He had already starved and neglected her siblings, so compassion for children was not an issue with Andreas. The man was abusive to his entire family.

After one hundred years the slaughter of six people on a cold, snowy night in 1922 still draws true crime fans and lovers of horror films. People tend to want clear cut answers to unsolved mysteries, however, sometimes we only get the known facts and our own conclusions.

The End

Memorial established at the former site of the Hinterkaifeck farm near Gröbern, Germany.

https://www.findagrave.com/memorial/158236156/andreas-gruber#

Front side   Back side

Funerial card for Hinterkaifeck victims. The maid, Maria Baumgartner was included with the family.

Bibliography

Unpublished Sources

Copies of subsequent articles, reports and reports kept in the state archives Augsburg and Munich were - unless otherwise noted - taken from the source collection available at http://www.hinterkaifeck.net/wiki.

Memo regarding the mechanic Albert Hofner and identification of the reuthaue by Georg Siegl, former servant at Hinterkaifeck, Munich, May 19, 1925.

Schrobenhausen District Court file in the guardianship of Josef Gruber, Vorm.-Verz. No. 216/1919 of September 30, 1919 (State Archives Munich, AG Schrobenhausen VV 216/1919).

Application by Bavarian State Police / Swabian Head Office for an arrest warrant to be issued against Anton Gump, Ingolstadt, May 7, 1952.

Application by the Augsburg Public Prosecutor's Office for an arrest warrant to be issued Anton Gump, Augsburg, May 2, 1952.

Security commissioner Georg Goldhofer reported that he had found the pocket knife, Hohenwart, March 31, 1923.

Criminal commissioner Georg Neuss reported to the Munich police department, Schrobenhausen, May 2, 1922.

Minutes of Senior Judge Johann Konrad Wiessner, Neuburg dated, April 4-5, 1922.

Report of Chief Criminal Inspector of the state police Xaver Meiendres on Hinterkaifeck homicide case, Sudelfeld [Bayrischzell], August 12, 1948.

Prosecutor's report Richard Pielmayer, Neuburg dated November 6, 1926.

Report of the investigating Chief Criminal Inspector Georg Reingruber, Munich, April 6, 1922.

Report from Public Prosecutor Ferdinand Renner to Chief Public Prosecutor Augsburg, Neuburg dated April 10, 1922.

Report from Public Prosecutor Ferdinand Renner to Chief Public Prosecutor Augsburg, Neuburg dated May 12, 1922.

Report from Public Prosecutor Ferdinand Renner to Chief Public Prosecutor Augsburg, Neuburg dated October 20, 1923.

Report of Criminal Inspector Martin Riedmayr on Lorenz Schlittenbauer, Munich, February 5,1931.

Report of forensic investigation by the Munich Police Department [Detective Superintendent Albert Mayer], Munich, April 10, 1922.

Report by Neuberg Prosecutor- telegraph to autopsy the body, Neuburg April 7, 1922.

Letter from Hans Anneser to the Public Prosecutor's office in Augsburg, Wettenhausen [Kammeltal municipality], February 25, 1949.

Letter from Sergeant Heinrich Nagel to the public prosecutor at the Neuburg District Court, on discovery of the reuthaue, Hohenwart, February 26, 1923.

Letter from the Schrobenhausen Gendarmerie Station to the Chief Public Prosecutor in the Augsburg Regional Court, Schrobenhausen, January 3, 1934.

Arrest warrant for Magdalena Schindler, Augsburg, May 3, 1952.

Interrogation Report Josef Betz, Munich, April 7, 1922.

Interrogation Report Anton Bichler, Gut Lindauhof (Althegnenberg community) [Fürstenfeldbruck District], May 4, 1922.

Interrogation Report Karl Bichler, Althegnenberg (in mayor's apartment, Johann Glück), May 4, 1922.

Interrogation Report Michael Bichler, Schrobenhausen, April 26, 1922. Interrogation Report Wenzeslaus Bley, Munich, August 8, 1930.

Interrogation Report Xaver Dersch, Pfaffenhofen, December 11, 1951.

Interrogation Report Johann Freundl, Gröbern, 17. December 1951.

Interrogation Report Sofie Fuchs, Gröbern, December 17, 1951.

Interrogation Report Sofie Fuchs, Gröbern, February 17, 1984.

Interrogation Report Georg Greger, Wangen, April 5, 1922.

Interrogation Report Bemhard Gmber, Munich, August 2, 1922.

Interrogation Report Anton Gump, Augsburg, May 10, 1952.

Interrogation Report Franziska Gump, Ingolstadt, May 28, 1952.

Interrogation Report Albert Hofner, Reichertshausen, May 15, 1925.

Interrogation Report Michael Huber, Gut Lindahof (Althegnenberg Community) [Fürstenfeldbruck District], May 4, 1922.

Interrogation Report Johann Kammer, Munich, August 1, 1930.

Interrogation Report Georg Kemer, Ortsangabe, November 27, 1951.

Interrogation Report Walburga Krammer, Schrobenhausen, December 18, 1933.

Interrogation Report Florentine Liebl, Augsburg, May 8, 1952.

Interrogation Report Sebastian Mayer, Flohenwart, April 26 1931.

Interrogation Report Josef Mayer, Waidhofen, January 10, 1952.

Interrogation Report Josef Mayer, Schrobenhausen, June 5, 1952.

Interrogation Report Heinrich Ney, Augsburg, January 19, 1953.

Interrogation Report Heinrich Ney, Kaufbeuren, March 20, 1953.

Interrogation Report Michael Plöckl (Sr.) Gröbern, December 17, 1951.

Interrogation Report Michael Pöll, Waidhofen, April 5, 1922.

Interrogation Report Kreszenz Rieger, Adelshausen [Karlskron], April 24, 1922.

Interrogation Reports Rieger | Hammer | Friedl, Munich, July 5, 1929.

Interrogation Report Kreszenz Rieger, Augsburg, December 9, 1933.

Interrogation Report August Ritzl, Augsburg, March 31 1952.

Interrogation Report Franziska Schäfer, Hinterkaifeck. April 5, 1922.

Interrogation Report Franziska Schafer and Josef Schäfer. Munich, June 9, 1925.

Interrogation Report Franziska Schäfer, Munich, May 2, 1932.

Interrogation Report Johann Schaupp and Maria Schaupp, Schrobenhausen, June 26, 1931.

Interrogation Report Kreszenz Schilling, Sattelberg, August 27, 1971.

Interrogation Report Magdalena Schindler, Freising, May 6, 1952.

Interrogation Report Hans Schirovsky and Eduard Schirovsky, Hinterkaif¬eck, April 5, 1922.

Interrogation Report Johann Schlittenbauer, Gröbern, January 10, 1952.

Interrogation Report Lorenz Schlittenbauer, Hinterkaifeck, April 5, 1922.

Interrogation Report Lorenz Schlittenbauer, Munich, March 30, 1931.

Interrogation Report Kreszenz Schmidt, born Rieger, Buttenwiesen [District of Dillingen on the Danube], July 9, 1952.

Interrogation Report Josef Schrätzenbarner, Hinterkaifeck, April 5, 1922.

Interrogation Report Josef Schrätzenbarner, Gröbern, December 17, 1951.

Interrogation Report Josef Schrittenlocher, Gröbern, December 17, 1951.

Interrogation Report Josef Schrittenlocher, Gröbern, July 1, 1952.

Interrogation Report Andreas Schwaiger, Gröbern, December 17 1951.

Interrogation Report [Tape recording] Andreas Schwaiger, Gröbern, July 4, 1980.

Interrogation Report Georg Siegl, Hohenried, April 27, 1922.

Interrogation Report Jakob Sigl, Waidhofen, April 5, 1922.

Interrogation Report Jakob Sigl, Schiltberg, January 10, 1952.

Interrogation Report Cecilia Starringer, Gröbern, April 5, 1922.

Interrogation Report Anton Strasser, Munich, May 23, 1924.

Interrogation Report Johann Walter, Waidhofen, April 28, 1922.

Interrogation Report Hans Yblagger, Bad Reichenhall, 19. February 1931.

Printed Sources and Literature

Aumann, Fritz: The Hinterkaifeck massacre, in; Swabian New Press from 04/2/1971 (http://www.hinterkaifeck.net/wiki).

Federal Court of Justice. Announcement from the press office no. 131/2012: conviction in the incest trial of Willmersbach is final, Karlsruhe August 20, 2012.

Koppel, Adolph J.: Der Gruber War's: Lückenlose Aufklärung Mordfall Hinterkaifeck (German Edition) Paperback – June 23, 2021

Leuschner, Peter: The Hinterkaifeck murder case. Traces of a mysterious crime, 3rd, revised and expanded edition, Hofstellen 2007 (cited in Leuschner, Mordfall).

Leuschner, Peter: Hinterkaifeck. Germany's most mysterious murder case, 1st edition, Hofstetten 2009 (quoted Leuschner, Hinterkaifeck).

Sueddeutsche Zietung   17th May 2010 Mysterious murder 1922 - Mystery about a seventh corpse   https://www.sueddeutsche.de/bayern/90-jahre-nach-der-tat-von-hinterkaifeck-moerderisches-mysterium-1.1321872 Stephen Mayr.

Gutmann, Josef: Major Fire in Gröbern, in: Schrobenhausener Wochenblatt from 11/6/1926 (http://www.hinterkaifeck.net/wiki).

Gutmann, Josef: The Horrific Crimes of Hinterkaifeck,: Schrobenhausener Wochenblatt from 02/81922 (http://www.hinterkaifeck.net/wiki).

Golla, Guido: Hinterkaifeck: Autopsie eines Sechsfachmordes: Books on Demand (August 18, 2016).

Hieber, Kurt Konrad: [Hinterkaifeck. On the trail of a murderer], TV report by ZDF. (Maynz) 1991 (quoted Hieber, [ZDF 1991]).

Hieber, Kurt Konrad: [The Hinterkaifeck Case. The real story behind Tannöd], TV report by ZDF, (Maynz) 2009 (quoted Hieber, [ZDF 2009]).

Bill James, Rachel McCarthy James (2017). The Man from the Train: The Solving of a Century-Old Serial Killer Mystery. NY: Scribner.

Lautenbacher, Johann: The Bloody Act of Hinterkaifeck : Augsburger Zeitung from 04/8/1922 (http://www.hinterkaifeck.net/wiki).

Leuschner, Peter: Hinterkaifeck. Germany's Most Mysterious Murder Case, 1st edition, Hofstetten 2009 (quoted Leuschner, Hinterkaifeck).

Leuschner, Peter: The Hinterkaifeck Murder Case. Traces of a Mysterious Crime, 3rd, revised and expanded edition, Hofstellen 2007 (cited in Leuschner, Mordfall).

Mayr, Stefan: Secret of a seventh corpse, in: Süddeutsche Zeitung from 03/11/2009 (http://\vww.hinterkaifeck.net/wiki).

Schrobenhausener Wochenblatt, No. 43 from 04/13/1922.

DER SPIEGEL, 7. Volume, No. 3 (14.01.1953).

Ulrich, Heinz / Gronefeld, Gerhard: I Know who the Killer is ..., in: Weltbild from May 5, 1952 (http://www.hinterkaifeck.net/wiki).

Ulrich, Heinz / Gronefeld, Gerhard: I know who the killer is ..., in: Weltbild from 05. May 1952 (http://www.hinterkaifeck.net/wiki).

Ulrich, Heinz / Gronefeld, Gerhard: They call me a murderer with no shadow of evidence! : Weltbild from 05. 06.1953 (http://www.hinterkaifeck.net/wiki).

Ulrich, Heinz: Summary of the Hinterkaifeck murder case, without location [Augsburg], o. Year number [1953] (State Archives Augsburg, IJs 244/52) (http://www.hinterkaifeck.net/wiki).

Ulrich, Heinz / Gronefeld, Gerhard: They Call Me a Murderer with No Trace of Evidence! : Weltbild from 06.51953 (http://www.hinterkaifeck.net/wiki).

Ulrich, Heinz: Summary of the Hinterkaifeck Murder Case, without location [Augsburg], Year number [1953] (State Archives Augsburg, IJs 244/52) (http://www.hinterkaifeck.net/wiki).

University of Applied Sciences for Public Administration and Justice in Bavaria [FHVR], Police Department, 2004/07 B: Final project report on the topic: Hinterkaifeck. A Murder Case With No End, Fürstenfeldbruck (June) 2007 (quoted FHVR, Hinterkaifeck).

Web Sites

https://www.hinterkaifeck.net/reader-ffb-bericht/
2007, 15 prospective detectives at the University of Applied Sciences for Administration and Law in Fürstenfeldbruck near Munich chose the Hinterkaifeck murder case for their final thesis.

Hinterkaifeck   Chadwick

www.ingramcontent.com/pod-product-compliance
Lightning Source LLC
Chambersburg PA
CBHW070107030426
42335CB00016B/2042